INTERNATIONAL MISSIONARY COUNCIL CENTENARY SERIES

Christian Mission in the Middle East

INTERNATIONAL MISSIONARY COUNCIL CENTENARY SERIES

Christian Mission in the Middle East

Ecumenical Perspectives

Edited by

Wilbert van Saane and John Holdsworth

First published 2024 by Regnum Books International
This edition is published under license from the World Council of Churches

Regnum is an imprint of the Oxford Centre for Mission Studies
St. Philip and St. James Church
Woodstock Road
Oxford, OX2 6HR, UK
www.regnumbooks.net

British Library Cataloguing in Publication Data
A catalogue record for this book is available from the British Library

ISBN: 979-8-8898-3865-4
eBook ISBN: 979-8-8898-3866-1

Typeset by Words by Design
www.wordsbydesign.co.uk

This series has been published with the financial support of EMW and CWME

Distributed by Fortress Press in the US, Canada, India, and Brazil

Series Preface

This series of books arises from a study process that marked the centenary of the International Missionary Council (IMC), founded in 1921 at Lake Mohonk, USA. It has its origin in the Commission on World Mission and Evangelism of the World Council of Churches, which wanted to celebrate the work of its historical predecessor IMC (1921-1961). In 2020, it therefore initiated a global and ecumenical study process, which was strongly supported by the Oxford Centre for Mission Studies (OCMS) in the UK and the Association of Protestant Churches and Missions in Germany (EMW) in Hamburg. The 18-month study process involved some 15 academic and ecumenical study centres or groups around the world, practically in all eight regions of the World Council of Churches, paying special attention to those sectors which were not represented at Lake Mohonk a hundred years earlier.

The International Missionary Council Centenary Series edited by the steering committee of the process in cooperation with the director of the CWME of the WCC presents the most interesting parts of the study process. The IMC was founded to foster mission cooperation and unity, and the study process wanted to identify important topics and challenges for mission and mission cooperation, not only in the past, even if the history of the IMC is to be celebrated, but also in the present and future. The steering committee of the study process was delighted to discover that some previously unheard voices have been heard through the process. Indeed, in order to honour the legacy of the IMC, the study process itself was implemented in an interactive and inclusive way that produced more mission cooperation and more unity among various actors in academy, church and mission bodies.

The volumes in the International Missionary Council Centenary Series present mainly, but not only, regional aspects and dimensions of world mission that has become polyphonic. The polyphonic character of mission opens and offers new common spaces for discussion and reflection on how all actors, churches, academy, mission bodies and transnational networks, can work together in creative and innovative ways, both in missiology and mission practice.

This Regnum Series builds on three foundational books that were generated by the study process and published by WCC Publications in 2022-23. A comprehensive Jubilee volume appeared as Risto Jukko ed., *Together in the Mission of God: Jubilee Reflections on the International Missionary Council*, Geneva: WCC Publications, 2022. Additionally, two mission studies anthologies gathered up the initial fruits of the study process: Risto Jukko ed., *A Hundred Years of Mission Cooperation: the Impact of the International Missionary Council 1921-2021*, Geneva: WCC Publications, 2022; and Risto Jukko ed., *The Future of Mission Cooperation: the Living Legacy of the International Missionary Council*, Geneva: WCC Publications, 2023. Now the Regnum Series offers a much more extensive harvest of the work completed by the study centres which collaborated in the IMC centenary study process.

The steering committee is delighted to be able to make the results of the study process accessible to a wider readership while recognising that opinions expressed in the book chapters are those of their authors and claim no wider authority.

Series Editors:

Marina Ngursangzeli Behera
Michael Biehl
Risto Jukko
Kenneth R. Ross
Tito Paredes
Peter Cruchley
Jingqin Gu

Contents

Introduction

John Holdsworth and Wilbert van Saane

The Middle East is the world's oldest mission field. It is where Christianity was born and so, by implication, this is the milieu in which its earliest expansion took place, and the place from which Christianity was first sent. There are those who feel that it has, therefore, a privileged place in the understanding of Christian theology. It contains historic churches that can trace their roots to the earliest times and who sometimes view with suspicion the versions of Christianity that are sent back from other parts, particularly of the western world. This is the home of orthodoxy as well as Orthodoxy.

But it has also a unique setting in the contemporary world. In the last hundred years and certainly since the dawn of the 20th century, it has experienced the displacement of peoples on a massive scale. It has experienced at least one attempt at ethnic cleansing in the Armenian genocide. It can recognize the results of colonialism even in the ways its national boundaries are drawn and the nation state model forced upon it. At the same time, it has seen incredible economic change thanks to the natural resources it is gifted with, particularly oil. Now it contains states that are arguably amongst the most ethnically diverse on earth. It has some of the earth's richest and most modern cities and economies.

It has also had its share of regional wars and conflict, sometimes associated with religious difference. The world's three great monotheistic religions derive from here and live together here with varying degrees of comfort. Alongside the rich cities, the refugee camps, ubiquitous in the region, and some dating back to 1948, bear witness in part to past and present suspicion of "the other." There is huge inequality in terms of income, education, employment chances and the place accorded to women throughout the region. Despite the influence of the global west, the region retains its familiar cultural hallmarks of welcome, hospitality, family cohesion and neighbourliness. One might say there could be no better context for Christian action, understanding and mission than this, but that needs to be nuanced by considering the region, its history, and its possibilities from the different perspectives that this volume offers.

The Making of This Book

Anniversaries are moments to look back and reflect on a journey. This book is the fruit of a study process occasioned by the centenary of the International Missionary Council, which was founded in 1921 and integrated in the World Council of Churches in 1961, continuing under the name Commission on World Mission and Evangelism (CWME) until the present. In various parts of the world, ad hoc regional study centres worked on the history of cooperation in mission. Almost all the chapters in this book were presented at meetings of the Middle East study centre in the period 2021-2022.

The invitation to form a study centre was issued by the CWME. The staff of the CWME felt a need to investigate the historical impact of cooperation in mission in different regions, and present-day opportunities for cooperation. Fostering regional and international cooperation was the mandate of the International Missionary Council when it was first established and continues to drive the ecumenical work of the CWME. The Middle East study centre reported to an international steering committee and was continuously aware that similar groups in other parts of the world were doing similar work. The group produced two reports: the first report traced the history of cooperation in mission in the Middle East and the second report mapped present challenges for the churches in their mission.[1]

In the Middle East, the Near East School of Theology in Beirut took the lead in forming a study centre, with advice from the Middle East Council of Churches. Scholars from the different ecclesial traditions–Eastern Orthodox, Oriental Orthodox, Catholic, and Protestant–were invited to contribute. Hence, we chose as subtitle for this book: "ecumenical perspectives." The subtitle should not be taken to mean that this volume is an expression of the views of official ecumenical bodies such as the Middle East Council of Churches. The views expressed here are those of the authors of the various chapters. Nevertheless, all authors have reflected on historical examples and possible avenues of cooperation in Christian mission. All chapters reflect a conviction that cooperation across denominations is indispensable for Christian mission in the interconnected 21st century Middle East. It should be noted that the authors have formulated their views in the English language – for most their second or third language – and that this would have been a different book had it been authored in the languages of the Middle East.

At an early stage, the Middle East study centre discussed a working definition of mission. The ecclesial traditions have quite different understandings of mission, some preferring terms such as "apostolate." Most members of the group felt comfortable with the five marks of mission that reached their final formulation at a meeting of the Anglican Consultative Council in Wales in 1990. These five marks have become the common understanding of mission in the Anglican Communion: (1) to proclaim the good news of the kingdom; (2) to teach, baptize, and nurture new believers; (3) to respond to human need by loving service; (4) to transform unjust structures of society, to challenge violence of every kind, and pursue peace and reconciliation; (5) to strive to safeguard the integrity of creation, and sustain and renew the life of the earth. Readers of this volume will discover that these marks are relevant to the context of the Middle East and are addressed by the churches on many levels.

---

[1] The first report was published in *A Hundred Years of Mission Cooperation: The Impact of the International Missionary Council 1921-2021*, ed. Risto Jukko (Geneva: WCC Publications, 2022), 237-269. The second report was published in *The Future of Mission Cooperation: The Living Legacy of the International Missionary Council*, ed. Risto Jukko (Geneva: WCC Publications, 2022), 61-88.

Mission in a Changing Landscape

Caleb Hutcherson and Brent Hamoud confront the reality of enforced displacement. 60 percent of the world's refugees are to be found here. Consequently, much of the churches' mission here has been concerned with meeting practical need. After charting the historical events that have led to the present situation, they turn to more fundamental questions about the nation state political arrangements that have defined them as refugees. They explore how ecumenical cooperation in mission can expose and challenge those underlying assumptions of contemporary political systems undergirding the cruelty of forced displacement. Examples of such cooperation include the American University of Beirut, now secularized but originally the Syrian Protestant College, training people in the skills needed to alleviate suffering. They offer further examples from Lebanon and Jordan. They conclude that the nation state template has much to answer for, and see hope in Christian mission that promotes new norms of identity and personhood.

John Holdsworth describes how the modern situation in the Anglican Diocese of Cyprus and the Gulf has prompted theological discussion about the kind of ecclesiology that can respond to it. Reflecting on the situation particularly in those Gulf States where Christian churches can operate relatively freely, he identifies the categories of diversity, open and generous hospitality and welcome as justice related categories that can act as building blocks for such a mission-based ecclesiology. Other potential categories include the settledness of chosen displacement as opposed to the exile of economic migrants from the Indian subcontinent, and how that contributes to discussion about questions of identity related to place. The issue of boundaries is particularly acute in this region and that too has theological depth.

The cultures, economies, and demographics of the Middle East are deeply affected by the ecological crisis. Some of the driest and hottest places on earth are found here. The military conflicts that raged in the 21st century were partially due to climate change and the scarcity of natural resources. The churches are only beginning to respond to this, but, as Rima Nasrallah demonstrates, they have rich liturgical traditions that can inspire their ecological mission. Their texts, rituals, and ascetic practices give expression to theologies that embrace the gifts of God's creation, including the land itself, which was sanctified by the incarnation. Thus, a new appreciation of the Middle Eastern liturgical traditions may unlock simpler, more sustainable, and joyful lifestyles that restore and heal creation.

Mission and Religious Diversity

The religious diversity of the Middle East has prompted much reflection on the relation between Christian mission and interfaith dialogue. This question is addressed by Elias Halabi, who offers insights from the history of the ecumenical movement. He argues that mission is not opposed to dialogue but may be characterized as "proclamation in dialogue." The ecumenical movement in the Middle East was well-positioned to explore the shape and role of Christian mission within a predominantly Islamic context. It did so not in isolation but in collaboration with Islamic communities, and also invited them to joint reflection on the Islamic concept of *da'wah*. Much progress was made and Elias Halabi reminds us of the fruit of these dialogues. They demonstrated the importance of commitment to one's faith, honesty, and the renunciation of hidden agendas in mission and *diakonia*. A strong tradition of institutional dialogue does not replace the living dialogue of everyday life but may serve as a model and a valve to defuse sectarian tensions that often flare up in response to political turmoil.

A fundamental question arising from the diversity, increasingly experienced throughout the region, is how to maintain Christ-centeredness in multi-cultural educational settings. Ziad Fahed writes about this from the perspective of Lebanon, though he believes his remarks have wider relevance. He highlights the importance placed on education in Lebanese culture and history, and notes that many educational establishments had Christian mission origins. His concern is that as the state becomes more involved on behalf of an increasingly diverse community, there is a challenge to the churches to present their teaching in schools in a way that is faithful to Christian tradition and yet acknowledges its diverse constituency.

He asks, "How does the Christian intellectual, academic tradition contribute to the nation's intellectual culture? In relation to that, how do Christian social and moral teaching contribute to the nation's development? How can those involved in Christian educational work, while respecting the ethos of each institution, develop and strengthen an ecumenical missionary spirit within each educational institution? And, finally, how can the churches play a constructive role within the schools and universities, helping them to remain faithful to their missionary call?" In answering his questions, he explores what a Christian institution should aspire to, and finds an example in Catholic Social teaching.

Missionary Actors

Antoine Al Ahmar and Garen Yosolkanian are the first to admit that "Monasticism and mission may seem mutually exclusive terms." It is surely only this region that they have contemporary currency. Of course, history tells us of the role of the monasteries in places like Britain and France in maintaining and spreading the gospel in both word and deed, but in the Middle East that is a present reality. This region is the cradle of Christian monasticism and has at times in its history maintained the faith in difficult times. Moreover, it is becoming more popular.

During the second half of the 20th century in Egypt for example there has been growth from seven Coptic monasteries with a handful of monks to fifty monasteries and thousands of monks. Examples, from many available, are taken from three traditions. Armenian monasticism has thrived following years of persecution and state sponsored atheism. Mission is intentional in the Maronite monasteries and education is a particular emphasis. As with monasteries of all traditions these places offer "a serene atmosphere of peace that many people are seeking in a permanently anxious world," and people visit them to catch a glimpse of what a consecrated life may look like. Melkite monasteries also have a role in education and in their contribution to academic theology and learning. Monasteries have maintained the faith, made a great contribution to Christian education and learning and have offered centres of liturgical excellence for their respective churches. So, they have contributed what in other cultures might be expected in part of cathedrals.

The historiography of Christian mission in the Middle East has often overlooked the role of women. Grace Al-Zoughbi reflects on the crucial role of Arab Protestant women in mission in the 20th century. She demonstrates the close connection between theological education and Christian mission. The increasing educational opportunities for women were often due to the efforts of (women) missionaries who empowered local women to engage in mission. She also argues that, the influence of western mission agencies notwithstanding, Protestant women had an authentic identity and contribution to theological education and mission. She tells the stories of women from Egypt, Syria and Lebanon, which demonstrate their pioneering and influential work.

The interplay between foreign agencies and local churches is explored by Asadour Manjrian who sketches the history of the Christian Endeavor movement in the Middle East. This youth movement was born in the United States and found a home in many parts of the world. In the Middle East, it was integrated in the youth work of the Armenian evangelical churches. Unlike other mission agencies, the Christian Endeavor groups relied entirely on local leadership and aimed to strengthen the churches and their mission among young people. As a result, they were never perceived as a western imposition and were able to respond to specific material and spiritual needs, such as caring for a generation of young genocide survivors. The spirituality of the Christian Endeavor movement proved flexible enough to be adopted by the local cultures, while at the same time remaining a source of renewal in worship and mission.

Christians in the Middle East may pay a high price for their commitment to mission, and even be martyred. There is a two-way relation between mission and martyrdom: mission may lead to martyrdom but martyrdom also inspires mission. The latter happens when Christian communities remember their martyrs and resolve to follow their examples. Wilbert van Saane reflects on martyrdom and mission in the light of four cases of martyrdom that have occurred in the 21st century. He observes that Christian martyrdom reveals a dedication to the lands and the communities of the Middle East. Martyrdom epitomises the sacramental presence of the Christian churches, which ultimately points to Christ and invites the diverse religious communities to peace and reconciliation.

It is our hope that this volume will help practitioners in mission in the Middle East to reflect on their calling and praxis. Many of the authors combine practical involvement with academic work and their reflections are informed by their direct experience of mission practice. The following chapters offer no quick fixes and 'how to' solutions. Rather, they invite readers to see past and present missionary practices in a new light and imagine new possibilities for ecumenical cooperation in mission. This is a book about old borders that have been crossed when hands were joined, and new borders that wait to be crossed by people working together in an ecumenical spirit.

Problems and Possibilities of Cooperation in Mission among (forcibly) Displaced People in the Middle East

Caleb Hutcherson and Brent Hamoud

"i want to go home
but home is the mouth of a shark
home is the barrel of a gun
and no one would leave home
unless home chased you to the shore"
Warsan Shire in "Home"

In her 2016 poem "Home" British-Somali poet Warsan Shire exposes the brutal deprivation and human agony of forced displacement. Home, for her, expresses feelings of both belonging to a place and dwelling within sites of memory and meaning, but it also exposes the dreaded violence, insecurity, and loss of control undermining the very core of the human experience. Throughout the piece Shire draws our attention to the trauma that comes when home and belonging – the natural basis of everyday life – are ripped away by displacement. "You only leave home when home won't let you stay."[1]

Shire wrote this intimate portrait of a personal and familial tragedy during the height of what was known as Europe's refugee and migration crisis in 2015-2016. During this period, some 5.2 million refugees and migrants had entered the European Union from Syria and Iraq, as well as many other countries, fleeing from violent conflict and war.[2] Yet that astonishing number of displaced people was only a portion of the total number of forcibly displaced Syrians alone, with nearly half of the country's population of 26 million forced into displacement. It was part of a wider regional crisis. As of 2017, 60 percent of the 23 million refugees in the world were located in the Middle East.[3] Without minimizing the individual experiences of crisis, the long, tragic history of human displacement both in the Middle East and elsewhere suggests that the disastrous displacement of people from their places is an enduring reality of human experience.

As a result of the prevalence and persistence of forced displacement in the Middle East, a great deal of Christian mission within this region has involved relief and development among forcibly displaced people. There is a long and complex story to be told about cooperation (and conflict) in mission between churches in the Middle East as they have sought to provide support to forcibly

---

[1] Warsan Shire, "Home," *Genius*, 13 March 2017, accessed 11 February 2023, https://genius.com/Warsan-shire-home-annotated.

[2] UNHCR, "Refugee Crisis in Europe: Aid, Statistics and News," accessed 11 February 2023, https://www.unrefugees.org/emergencies/refugee-crisis-in-europe/.

[3] Jordi Tejel and Ramazan Hakkı Öztan, "The Special Issue: 'Forced Migration and Refugeedom in the Modern Middle East' Towards Connected Histories of Refugeedom in the Middle East," *Journal of Migration History* 6:1 (February 2020), 6. https://doi.org/10.1163/23519924-00601002.

displaced people during the past century. That said, the historical context within which this mission activity has taken place is inseparably linked to the emergence and establishment of the modern nation-state system, which redrew the outline of the region (and the world) and invariably forced people into displacement. As a consequence, the story of forced displacement and modern missions in the Middle East must be considered with reference to the nation-state as a historical force shaping the way we understand and respond to the crisis. It has cemented the global environment in which categories of out-of-placeness (like refugees and stateless persons) have crystallized.

In this chapter our purpose is to consider how the phenomenological human reality of forced displacement in the Middle East has expanded into a complex dilemma related to people and place with severe legal, sociological, and spiritual entanglements, and from that analysis offer suggestions for how ecumenical cooperation in mission might expose dimensions of the human crisis and identify opportunities to engage missionally.

To do so, we begin by describing the nature of forced displacement in the Middle East and tracing the role of nation-states in creating displacement preceding and during the period 1921-2021, which marks the centenary of the International Missionary Council (IMC), which in 1961 became the Commission on World Mission and Evangelism (CWME) within the World Council of Churches. The IMC/CWME was a significant instrument in global Christian missionary cooperation. Through this analysis, we argue that contemporary understandings of forced displacement are grounded in the nation-state system, which is underpinned by assumptions about people, places, how belonging is enjoyed, and displacement is experienced. We then describe and analyze the possibilities and problems of cooperation in mission with and among forcibly displaced people in the Middle East. Following this, we consider how ecumenical cooperation in mission can expose and challenge underlying assumptions of contemporary political systems undergirding the cruelty of forced displacement. Based on this analysis, we bring forward suggestions for ways in which ecumenical cooperation in mission with and among forcibly displaced people can prophetically critique systems fostering such exclusion.

Forced Displacement in the Middle East: Defining Who Counts as a Refugee

Forced displacement encompasses a general human condition of placelessness but, for better or worse, the modern political realities have crafted technical terms to define types of displacement. These can be both helpful in articulating circumstances and problematic in dehumanizing individuals with impersonal labels. Prevailing categories that we use today have developed through the codification of international law and proven rather durable in framing within pragmatic and legal frameworks, statuses of the displaced. The most common of these technical categories are refugees,[4] internally displaced people,[5] and asylum seekers.[6] Each of these terms is used technically to distinguish a nonnormative legal situation in reference to the nation-state, all of which point to a general experience of placelessness. Each category identifies technical sets of vulnerability and marginalization; all point to unquestionable need for a remedy against placelessness, whether that be a new place to call home or a return to the old home with guarantees of security and protection. In no circumstance is the displacement in view here a matter of preference. Rather, it is a plight of desperate necessity because, as Matthew Gibney writes:

> if forced to return home or remain where they are, they would – as a result of either the brutality or inadequacy of their state – be persecuted or seriously jeopardize their physical security or vital subsistence needs.[7]

Gibney's expansive definition points to the loss of place and agency underlying the condition of forced displacement. In doing so, it foregrounds the violation of people's ability to shape their own lives with regard to mobility and pursuing livelihoods, in addition to undermining people's sense of place and belonging.[8] This framework includes stateless people – those who reside in a state but have been excluded from a nationality and denied formal membership to any nation-state community.[9] Recognizing the way human displacement includes elements of degraded personhood and unsettled status is critical for

---

[4] Article I of the UN Refugee Convention (1951) uses three criteria to designate whether a person is a refugee or not: "1) has a well-founded fear of persecution because of their race, religion, nationality, membership in a particular social group, or political opinion; 2) are outside their country of origin; and 3) are unable or unwilling to avail themselves of the protection of that country, or return there, because of their fear of persecution," as discussed by Rupen Das and Brent Hamoud, *Strangers in the Kingdom: Ministering to Refugees, Migrants, and the Stateless* (Carlisle: Langham Global Library, 2017), 17.

[5] Internally displaced persons (IDP) are those who are forced away from their place, but who have not crossed an international border. There is no international law that protects them. Ibid., 18.

[6] Asylum seekers are potential refugees, based on "have(ing) left their country and … seeking protection (asylum) in another because they feel threatened in their home country. If their application is accepted…they become a legal refugee and have access to all entitled benefits and protections." Ibid.

[7] Matthew J. Gibney, *The Ethics and Politics of Asylum: Liberal Democracy and the Response to Refugees* (Cambridge: Cambridge University Press, 2004), 7.

[8] See Linsey Kingston's analysis of displacement as a threat to people's rights to "place and purpose that make a life of human dignity possible" in Kingston, *Fully Human: Personhood, Citizenship, and Rights* (New York: Oxford University Press, 2019), 3. Understanding this dynamic helps sensitize analysis to the complexities that inform the forcedness of displacement for those who are displaced.

[9] As such, stateless people cannot be recognized as "refugees," despite experiencing all of the violence of forced displacement. See Das and Hamoud, *Strangers*, 19; and Sari Hanafi, "Forced Migration in the Middle East and North Africa," in *The Oxford Handbook of Refugee and Forced Migration Studies*, ed. Elena Fiddian-Qasmiyeh (Oxford: Oxford University Press, 2014), 585-586.

understanding the human dimensions permeating problems of forced displacement in the Middle East and globally.

Displacement in the Middle East has been driven by various causes all of which result in individuals finding themselves stuck in broken relationships with their places. Sari Hanafi explains some of the driving causes of forced displacement in the 20th and 21st centuries from and within the Middle East, which include:

> …colonial experiences (as in the case of Palestinians expelled from the territory which became Israel), post-colonial contexts (such as Sahrawi and Kurdish refugees), civil war (Lebanese and Syrian refugees), and conflict and post-conflict situations (Iraqi refugees).[10]

Human displacement in the Middle East flows in multiple directions. Forced displacement *from* the Middle East, of course, is acknowledged in the above discussion. But forced migration also occurs *to* the Middle East, as a result of causes similar to those that drive people away. These include genocide, as was the case of the Armenians who fled to Lebanon and other parts of the Middle East in the early 20th century, and European Jews fleeing to Palestine in the period prior to, during, and immediately after World War II, and inter- and intrastate conflict. Recent examples include Sudanese and Yemeni people migrating to Egypt and other parts of the Middle East due to conflict or economic hardship in their countries. In these ways, the Middle East can be described as a vortex of forced displacement, with refugees moving to, within, and from the region.

In addition to these overt forms of conflict displacing people from their homelands, there are also various forms of more subtle violence that, based on Gibney's definition above, also might be understood as forcing people into displacement in the Middle East in ways that render them vulnerable in their placelessness. For instance, Sari Hanafi points to the experiences of people groups marked by non-citizenship and statelessness, saying:

> the region has also witnessed intersecting processes of forced displacement and forced sedentarization of mobile and nomadic populations for whom movement and mobility are central parts of their lives and livelihoods.[11]

As a result of discriminatory national policies, groups of people in the Middle East have been marginalized and denied claims to their homelands despite having never migrated from their historical locations. Stateless people have been deprived of a nationality and often blocked from any pathway towards citizenship. They are left "unable to rely on their country of nationality for protection" and live within a severe condition in which they are effectively displaced from the world altogether, existing in the world without enjoying formal membership to any part of it.[12] Acknowledging that violence may be acute (open conflict) or more structural (slow-burning economic deterioration or institutional exclusion based on blatant discrimination) points to a spectrum of

---

[10] Ibid., 585.

[11] Ibid.

[12] Das and Hamoud, *Strangers*, 19.

severity to the causes that force displacement. Likewise, the displacement itself never produces a general human condition but a range of realities subjected to unlimited numbers of variables both easing and intensifying the complications of placelessness.

Experiences of feeling displaced are on the rise among regional populations in general, as demonstrated by various polls within the Middle East measuring growing discontentedness of residents towards their national residence. For example, a poll conducted in 2021 shows that a significant majority of Lebanese youth want to leave their country, a sentiment shared by similarly high percentages of youth in many other Middle Eastern countries.[13] While the same surveys have recorded a decreasing interest in emigration among citizens of other countries, such as Jordan, Egypt, and Kuwait, the migrant populations in these countries (e.g. Sudanese in Egypt, Syrians in Jordan) report high interest in emigrating. That said, more than armed conflict or security issues, economic factors are the top driver of migration in nearly every country in the Middle East and North Africa.[14] This results in an unsettling dynamic in which Middle Eastern states host large refugee populations among a national population that is increasingly disconnected with their homelands and eager to depart to new locales. The result is a multidimensional dissatisfaction with people and their places resulting in instability and growing threats to social cohesion.

In view of the complexity of forced displacement, we note that some of the most common terms used to categorize the forcibly displaced such as *refugee, forced migrant, undocumented migrant, illegal alien,* and *internally displaced persons* all carry essential limitations. Scholars in the field of migration studies point to the inherent values and judgments that these labels communicate.[15] They are legal, political, and social constructions that risk obscuring the human identity of those categorized.[16] A shift has been made towards using terms emphasizing and exploring agency in mobility as a more useful category (e.g. forced migration, forced displacement, asylum seeker, stateless, etc.). Nevertheless, in defining these legal categories of displacement, it is critical to appreciate the human stories to which they point and rise above the way our system of nation-states subsumes these rigid, impersonal categories in the first

[13] "Half of Lebanese Consider Migrating," Arab Barometer website (Princeton University, 2022), accessed 28 September 2022: https://www.arabbarometer.org/2022/04/what-lebanese-citizens-think-about-migration/; Sally Farhat. "Lebanese Youths Seek a Brighter Future Abroad amid Economic, Political Crises," *France 24*, 26 April 2022. Accessed 28 September 2022, https://www.france24.com/en/middle-east/20220426-lebanese-youths-seek-out-a-brighter-future-abroad-amid-economic-political-crises

[14] Mohamed Abufalgha, "Public Views of Migration in MENA," Arab Barometer website (Princeton University, 2022) 6, accessed 28 September 2022, https://www.arabbarometer.org/wp-content/uploads/ABVII_Migration_Report-EN.pdf.

[15] Roger Zetter, "More Labels, Fewer Refugees: Remaking the Refugee Label in an Era of Globalization," *Journal of Refugee Studies* 20 (2007), 172–92.

[16] Daniel G. Groody, "Crossing the Divide: Foundations of a Theology of Migration and Refugees," *Theological Studies* 70:3 (September 2009), 642. https://doi.org/10.1177/004056390907000306.

place.[17] This claim is more significant than it may sound; it can undergird new paradigms for understanding the very nature of personhood and place within our contemporary world. Casting stringent definitions on who counts as displaced and how their displacement can be conceptualized is a matter of technicalities bound up with the modern nation-state system. Human displacement has existed at all times of human history, but the emergence of the nation-state has set the parameters for which the complexities are framed and solutions are imagined. Crises of displaced peoples are inherently crises of the form and function of the nation-state.

Considering Nation-States: The System That Defines Displaced People

Historical developments of the 19th and 20th century effectively brought about a transition from a world ruled by empires to a systematic global ordering of nation-states (although not without strong imperial impulses). Consequently, the modern nation-states of the Middle East emerged as the normative way of ordering territories and peoples. In doing so, this new system of organizing territories and people created the rigid legal and political parameters within which modern human displacement is understood and defined. Though this process involved supremely complex sets of variables and interactions playing out at all levels, two historical events stand out as flashpoints driving the shape of the contemporary status quo. The first of these is the First World War when surges of nationalism, imperial rivalries, deadly international conflict, and declining empire powers – particularly that of the Ottoman Empire – led to a reimagined world map drawn by global powers. New states were delineated, oftentimes under colonial patronage, that would become the seeds of our global community of nation-states.[18]

Few political and territorial landscapes were changed as dramatically in the post-World War I global ordering as the Middle East. After centuries of direct Ottoman rule, people and places across the Middle East were demarcated by Great Britain and France (with the agreement of imperial Russia) through the secret Sykes-Picot agreement in 1916. The borders determined by this agreement divided lands that were home to extraordinarily diverse people, including Arabs, Armenians, Assyrians, Chaldeans, Turks, and Jews. While there is debate about the role of these artificial[19] borders in driving subsequent conflicts in the Middle East, what is clear is that the resulting political institutions failed to capture the fluid, cosmopolitan realities of people, histories, political aspirations, and cultures.[20] While not attributing undue agency to the Anglo-French in the formation of Middle Eastern nation-states, the nation-state borders created by

---

[17] Dorottya Nagy, "Minding Methodology: Theology-Missiology and Migration Studies," *Mission Studies* 32:2 (June 2015), 31. https://doi.org/10.1163/15733831-12341401.

[18] Peter Gatrell, *The Making of the Modern Refugee* (Oxford: Oxford University Press, 2013), 25ff.

[19] Admittedly, all borders are arbitrary at some level.

[20] Aslı Bâli, "Sykes-Picot and 'Artificial' States," *AJIL Unbound* 110 (2016), 115–19. doi:10.1017/S2398772300002919.

these mandate powers divided human communities, such as tribes, religious groups, and ecclesial bodies. These political frameworks continue to undergird much of the region's human displacement challenges. In this new arrangement, people were displaced, as Hannah Arendt made crystal clear, "not because of what they had done or thought, but because of what they unchangeably were – born into the wrong kind of race or the wrong kind of class ."[21]

The second historical event of note is the Second World War and its aftermath. Concepts and practices conceived in the wake of WWI were crystalized into the current global system of nation-states and nationalities commonplace in our world today. The conflict inflicted an unparalleled scale of (primarily European) forced migration leading to high-level efforts to determine the relational dynamic of people and places within innovative legal and theoretical parameters of the nation-state and nationality. Examples of these kinds of efforts can be seen in the move to create nation-states via the UN Partition Plan for Palestine as a solution for displacement.[22] In fact, a host of international organizations, conventions, and human rights theories that shape the way we think about human displacement today trace their roots to this time.[23] These efforts advanced the ways in which people are protected in times of humanitarian crisis and codified international norms to bring durable situations to problems such as displacement, but the underlying problems of the nation-state have remained.

History is never simple or static, and we must avoid the temptation to minimize complexities or resort to reductionist explanations about how global events have unfolded and social and political systems have taken shape. It is imperative to handle historical narratives carefully when applying them to people and events, and this is especially the case when discussing religious experiences. This is particularly the case for Christians in the Middle East during a tumultuous past century as events related to the end of the Ottoman Empire, implementation of European colonial mandates, nation-state independence, commission of the State of Israel and massive dispossession of Palestinians, Cold War political manoeuvring, US military interventions and invasions, and a host of regional and national wars and civil conflicts have rattled landscapes at all levels and unleashed widespread human suffering. Tragically, conflict and turmoil have an uncanny tendency to create new cases of human displacement while making ongoing cases harder and harder to resolve.

The causes of forced displacement vary, but the outcome is similar: people's sense of emplacement has been severely disrupted, and as a result they suffer harrowing predicaments of non-belonging. Fundamentally, forced displacement disrupts the sense of place, purpose, and belonging of those who are displaced. As such, it is both a complex legal dilemma and one of the most pervasive forms of cruelty exacted on humans. As chronic to the human experiences as

---

[21] Hannah Arendt, *The Origins of Totalitarianism*, 2nd ed. (New York: Meridian, 1958), 267, 294.

[22] See "United Nations Special Committee on Palestine: Report to the General Assembly: Volume 1," 3 September 1947, 51, A/364(SUPP), accessed February 13, 2023: https://undocs.org/A/364(SUPP).

[23] Gatrell, *Making*, 85-87.

displacement may be, the contemporary realities of the nation-state make our current understandings and responses to the crisis particular in ways that can both extend protections to people in need and exacerbate hardships locking individuals into their plights of placelessness.

Forcibly Displaced People: Inadequacies of Nation-State Solutions

The region of the Middle East has been fundamentally shaped by forced displacement in the past 100 years, and especially as a result of the two World Wars. Solutions to displacement in this region are as varied as its causes. More problematically, however, these solutions are also linked to the historical development of the nation-state as the primary framework for organizing people and absorbing them into national status with their territories of residence.

As long as people's legal relationships to places are determined by the institutional rigidity embedded in the current global system of nation-states, people who find themselves forced from their places (or denied a place from birth) will be at risk of overwhelming exclusion. Middle Eastern history demonstrates how unforgiving the modern nation-state arrangement can be for those removed from their homes. Take for instance the experience of many ethnic Armenians and Syriacs (Sayfo) fleeing Turkish genocide early in the 20th century. Masses were forced to flee their historic homelands in the Ottoman provinces and Mesopotamian territories, but their relocations, though terrible ordeals, were aided by loose legal structures and fluid borders (or no borders at all) allowing them relocate and settle in new locations and enter the social fabric of their new contexts by taking on the nationality of countries like Syria and Lebanon.

This experience, however, starkly contrasts with the mass displacement of Palestinians in the middle of the 20th century. By this time, the Middle East had been ordered into its independent nation-state structure and pathways to formal integration into new places was severely blocked, with the Kingdom of Jordan being the unique example of where Palestinians were granted some degree of naturalization into their new places of residency. The widespread rejection of *tawteen* (Arabic for resettlement) and prioritization of a "right of return" as encoded by the new refugee rights actually has led to the perpetuation of the brutality of displacement for what are now multiple generations of Palestinian refugees.[24] Though the sociological variables bound up in these two cases studies are thick, the varying experiences illuminate profound insights into the gravity of the nation-state's tendency to lock individuals into spirals of displacement.

Debate continues at the national level in Middle Eastern states about whether formal refugee camps, informal settlements, integration, or forced repatriation are the best way to handle displaced people. The result in all cases is the definition and assignment of place and belonging based on nation-state identities. Thus, while these statuses of refugee and asylum seeker have the potential to offer some protections, rights, and provisions, they also perpetuate,

---

[24] Hanafi, "Forced," 591.

even legitimize, marginalization and displacement by rigidly designating outsiders as others subjected to degrees of exclusion.

There is much more that could be said about the violence of forced displacement by simply tracing the wide range of displacement situations in the Middle East, and considering the causes, experiences, and responses from various perspectives. In the next section, however, we focus on the responses of churches in mission among forcibly displaced people.

Mission among Forcibly Displaced People: Problems and Possibilities in Practice

Due to this long history and wide range of experiences of forced displacement from, to, and within the Middle East, Christian mission in this region has, by necessity, been intertwined with ministering to the humanitarian needs that accompany forced displacement. To that point, Keith Watenpaugh argues, the modern humanitarian project and its associated organizations were not simply linked with, but rather birthed out of, Christian missions within the region of the Middle East "as methods of evangelism gave way almost entirely to addressing the suffering of human beings and developing institutions for their care, social development, and higher education."[25] That is not to say that churches were not involved in this work, but rather that this humanitarian aspect of Christian mission in this region was so significant and widespread among missionaries and churches in response to the plight of forcibly displaced peoples that it fostered patterns of ecumenical cooperation and generated many of the humanitarian organizations that we know of today.[26] Tracing this history, Okkenhaug and Summerer affirm that "one of the central activities of mission-related humanitarianism from the 1860s onward, concerned the question of relief and refugees of the Middle East, due to the repetitive nature of forced migration since the 1850s, producing an expertise still relevant today."[27] In this way, meeting the needs of forcibly displaced people in the Middle East has actually shaped humanitarian work into what we know it as today.

That being the case, it is important to recognize other factors involved in humanitarian work among the displaced that also contribute to reshaping the goals and practices of missionary enterprises in part due to ecumenical cooperation. One exemplar of this transformation of an institution's goals due to cooperation in mission is the American University of Beirut (AUB). Founded in 1866 as the Syrian Protestant College, the post-World War I circumstances of the school were one of deep debt, financial and currency crisis, and tremendous

---

[25] Keith David Watenpaugh, *Bread from Stones. The Middle East and the Making of Modern Humanitarianism* (Oakland, CA: California University Press, 2015), 18.

[26] Inger Marie Okkenhaug and Karène Sanchez Summerer, "Introduction," in *Christian Missions and Humanitarianism in The Middle East, 1850-1950: Ideologies, Rhetoric, and Practices*, ed. Inger Marie Okkenhaug and Karène Sanchez Summerer, vol. 11, Leiden Studies in Islam and Society (Leiden: Brill, 2020), 6-8.

[27] Ibid., 12.

humanitarian needs of both students and the surrounding community.[28] This was due, in part, to a cooperative partnership brought together by the Near East Relief that involved the Rockefeller Foundation (RF) providing the needed funding to AUB and other Near East colleges in order for them to further develop medical services in order to provide relief and aid to refugee populations.[29] This partnership with the RF prioritized partnering with secularized institutions. Additionally, AUB experienced pressure to develop a more secular institutional outlook through donations aimed at providing scholarships for refugee students.[30] While various other drivers also contributed to the secularization of AUB, the cooperative partnerships this Protestant missionary institution undertook in order to fund humanitarian work and relief among displaced people played a part in its secularization.

In contrast, examples of ecumenical cooperation in mission among and with forcibly displaced people can also be found, even in the contemporary situation. In research exploring contemporary Jordanian Anglican church leaders' attempts to discourage Syrian and Iraqi Christian refugees in Jordan from leaving the region, Lucy Schouten's research uncovers some of this ecumenical cooperation and mixing, whereby Christian refugees from various denominations are welcomed and integrated.[31] She argues that a distinct self-understanding of Middle Eastern Christianity among these church leaders contributes to cooperation in an attempt to stem emigration of Christian refugees from this region. Likewise, various multi-denomination faith-based organizations in Lebanon have expanded their relief work among Palestinian, Syrian, and Iraqi refugees, as well as stateless peoples such as the Dom, in response to the horrendous inadequacy of the state's response.[32] Alongside this, some denominations who had been adverse to ecumenical cooperation historically, such as Lebanese Baptists, demonstrate the potential for profound transformation towards more ecumenical cooperation that can come through church-based humanitarian work among and with forcibly displaced people.[33] Recent research captures an insider perspective of transformation through the critical relief work being done among forcibly displaced Syrians by Lebanese Baptist churches that previously avoided all humanitarian work as a distraction from their main objective of evangelism.[34] As a result, denominational organizations have

---

[28] Stephen Penrose, Jr., *That They May Have Life: The Story of the American University of Beirut 1866-1941* (Princeton: Princeton University Press, 1941), 167-169.
[29] See Philippe Bourmaud "Missionary work, secularization, and donor dependency: Rockefeller-Near East Colleges Cooperation after World War I (1920–1939)," in *Christian Missions and Humanitarianism in The Middle East, 1850-1950*, 161-164.
[30] Ibid., 168.
[31] Lucy Schouten, "Why Church Leaders Discourage Christians from Leaving Jordan: An Anti-Emigration Perspective," *Exchange* 49:3–4 (November 2020), 341.
[32] Note the expanding relief and development work of faith-based organizations such as Life Agape, Youth for Christ, Embrace the Middle East, Caritas, and World Vision.
[33] See Melanie E. Trexler, *Evangelizing Lebanon: Baptists, Missions, and the Question of Cultures* (Waco, TX: Baylor University Press, 2016), 35-37.
[34] Elie Haddad, "Cultivating Missional Ecclesiology for the Local Baptist Church in Lebanon" (PhD diss., Vrije Universiteit Amsterdam, 2021), 179ff; See also Kathryn

expanded their cooperation in ministry beyond denominational boundaries. These patterns of mission among and with forcibly displaced people actualize cooperation across denominational and national boundaries.

That being the case, fundamentalist and conservative theologies among Middle Eastern churches still perpetuate territorialism and competition in mission. Historically, some denominational ideologies have led church leaders and missionaries to reject ecumenical agreements and interdenominational cooperation in work among refugees, only cooperating with other associations and societies from within the same denomination.[35] This hesitancy to engage in ecumenical cooperation was present not only among evangelicals but also historical Christian denominations in the Middle East.[36] As a result, nation-state assumptions coupled with the historical suffering experienced along these lines of demarcation still impact church practices and activities with and among the displaced. For example, often for pragmatic reasons, many evangelical churches (not just Baptists) held separate Sunday services (either by time or location) for Lebanese and Syrians refugee communities, resulting in perpetuating already-present divisions.[37] Even when addressed by leadership, these kinds of exclusionary divisions continue to pattern the various services offered to refugee populations.

This territorialism and bordering extend to church practices related to support and aid distribution among displaced people. Drawing again on the Lebanese context for an example, due to waning international attention on the Lebanese economic crisis and the subsequent lack of funding, many Lebanese churches have had to limit the number of beneficiaries of financial or food aid. As a result, some churches resort to prioritizing distribution first to those who are "in the family" of the church, before extending donations to affiliations outside the church. In other cases, beneficiaries are determined by ratios so that one nationality is prioritized over other nationalities, rather than prioritizing aid based on need. Practically, these kinds of arrangements create informal social contracts where forcibly displaced beneficiaries of church-based aid understand that particular nationalities or church affiliation is required to receive aid. This means, for example, that it is much easier to get help from a Lebanese Baptist church if you are Lebanese, Baptist, evangelical, or Christian, in that order. While these policies are intended to foster aid to those in need, or for those who fall through the "gaps" of international organizations' policies, they carry with them assumptions patterned on nation-state systems of division and exclusion.

Secular, humanitarian aid organizations rightly draw attention to the danger of religious abuse due to the power imbalance between distributor and

---

Kraft, "Faith and Impartiality in Humanitarian Response: Lessons from Lebanese Evangelical Churches Providing Food Aid," *International Review of the Red Cross* 97:897–898 (June 2015), 22-23. https://doi.org/10.1017/S1816383115000570.

[35] Trexler, *Evangelizing*, 37.

[36] Wilbert van Saane. "Middle East Study Centre Historical Report," in *A Hundred Years of Mission Cooperation: The Impact of the International Missionary Council 1921-2021*, ed. Risto Jukko (Geneva: WCC Publications, 2022), 237-269.

[37] Haddad, "Cultivating," 182.

beneficiary.[38] In many of the church- and faith-based networks mentioned above, training has been offered to help churches become more aware of the problems with proselytization and conditionality, and find ways of mitigating this kind of conditionality.[39] Churches, in turn, emphasize the importance of dignity and relationship in aid distribution among displaced people. Nevertheless, prejudicial practices continue to creep into church-based humanitarian aid among forcibly displaced people in Middle Eastern churches today, and risks perpetuating power disparities and territorialism between churches, as well as between churches-as-distributors and forcibly-displaced-as-beneficiaries.[40] These experiences point to theologies embedded in the mission activities of churches in their humanitarian service with and among forcibly displaced people that maintain territorialist and discriminatory tendencies. These tendencies mimic the nation-state policies that define who is in and out, marginalizing people, and amplifying the violence of displacement. If cooperation in mission is to contribute to the welfare of forcibly displaced people, rather than amplifying their displacement, the underlying assumption of the nation-state paradigm requires further theological scrutiny.

Mission with the Forcibly Displaced: Subverting the Status-Quo by Promoting Personhood and Place

Surveying the past 100 years of ecumenical cooperation in mission in the Middle East illuminates fascinating global historical developments and their profound human implications. This period has witnessed the solidification of the nation-state as the global world order forged out of the trials of world wars and postcolonial conflicts. The world we know now is marked by political borders, nationality statuses and passports, and systems of international law which profess grand policy standards but often fail to penetrate nation-state sovereignty to apply to people in their situations. Though human displacement has always been a part of the human experience, current conditions have made the problems of displacement increasingly complex and harder to escape. The movement of people is not regarded as a matter of individuals and communities participating in the human tradition of migration but rather a problem, a threat, that must be managed by legal systems operating at national, regional, and global levels. The dominance of the nation-state has indeed helped elevate human rights and personal liberties/protections to historic levels, but its entrenchment also created new categories of "misplaced" people who are assigned debilitating labels such as refugee, stateless, and other forms of noncitizen. Certainly, this rigid classification of territory and people is unlike anything seen before in the human experience, and contradicts the basic principles of Christian theology and ethics.

---

[38] Kraft, "Faith," 10; ICRC Code of Conduct, Statement 3.

[39] Ibid., 17-19.

[40] Recent research among Syrians in Lebanon found that 70 percent had not received humanitarian aid in the past year. See Yasmin Kayali, "Syrian Refugees in Lebanon Need Help and Protection, Not More Pressure to Leave," *The New Humanitarian*, 18 January 2022, accessed 15 February 2023, https://www.thenewhumanitarian.org/opinion/2022/1/18/Syrian-refugees-Lebanon-help-protection-pressure-leave.

Human division is primordial, but the way delineation is politically instituted today is a modern innovation posing a set of truly phenomenal challenges for churches to operate within (and around).

Churches are uniquely situated within the contemporary nation-state system to serve human need in responsive, practical ways that promote human personhood. Their historic presence stretching back to previous eras predating present-day nation-state borders has fostered locally rooted, humanitarian communities existing across transnational networks. Moreover, churches have the theological resources needed to transcend the nation-state paradigm both in self-perception and in ecclesial polity. Historic ecclesial communities like the Armenian Orthodox in Lebanon already embody this trans-border alternative, seeking to connect both its local and diaspora community as members of the community wherever they go. Though churches have adapted to fit the modern reality of nation-states, they have the capability to operate outside of such institutions and the national loyalties that go with them. In the areas of practical life undermined by displacement (things like securing housing, earning livelihoods, accessing education, receiving medical treatment), churches fill gaps by providing vital services to ease suffering and sustain life in challenging times. This is well recognized, but just as important are the rituals of living, the sacred elements that give life meaning. Blessing marriages, celebrating births, memorializing and burying the deceased – churches can serve the human needs of people in the absence of or even in opposition to the state. All practical and spiritual ministry to the marginalized convey, when done sincerely as to Christ, a type of subversive statement honouring human dignity and dismissing the dehumanization of a systematic world. It amplifies a citizenry of heaven above the national confines of our global order.

Based on this description of church practices, it is also worthwhile to consider the theological resources available in the trans-border, nation-state defying practices of the Middle Eastern churches described above. Over against the nation-state paradigm, which has led to division and displacement, many Middle Eastern churches hold a theology in which the attachment to the land (rather than a nation) plays an important role. Middle Eastern theological reflection connects the people with the land as a gift and a trust from God.[41] This is so, not in spite of the Bible, but because migration and displacement (often forced) is a fundamental motif woven throughout the biblical record.[42] Looking to theologies of migration – not merely theology about caring for migrants, but looking to experiences of migration as a source of talk about the mystery of God – holds potential to critique Christian nationalism and sectarian tendencies. They can also help to "bridge the gap" between migration studies and theology.[43]

[41] See Munther B. I. Isaac, "From Land to Lands, from Eden to the Renewed Earth: A Christ-Centred Biblical Theology of the Promised Land" (PhD diss., Middlesex University, 2014), https://eprints.mdx.ac.uk/13711/.

[42] Andrew F. Walls, "Mission and Migration: The Diaspora Factor in Christian History," in *Global Diasporas and Mission*, ed. Chandler H. Im and Amos Yong, volume 23 Regnum Edinburgh Centenary Series (Oxford: Regnum, 2014), 19-20.

[43] Groody, "Crossing," 641-642.

Furthermore, the ecclesiology of Middle Eastern churches holds potential. Examples of these ecclesiologies include Orthodox churches and their Catholic (Uniate) offshoots that are organized by regional patriarchates, as well as for Protestant churches that prioritize a conception of the church as invisible and spiritual. Both of these ecclesiologies carry inherently transborder notions that challenge the exclusive focus on solutions for displacement based on the nation-state paradigm.

In countless ways, faith communities are uniquely positioned to respond to the numerous areas in which the current world order fails to manage the inherently dynamic, global, and fluid human experience embedded in humanity. As nation-states continue to negotiate their place and assert their authority in a rapidly changing world (oftentimes violently), churches occupy promising local and global orientations equipping them to respond to human needs by transgressing the authority of borders. A willingness to cooperate ecumenically – that is, across denominational "borders" – expands churches' capability to mitigate the harshness of nation-state borders (and the border mentalities that seek to preserve them at the expense of displaced people). For churches that span borders, their presence calls into question the nature of an international order that designates and defines individual lives within inflexible (border)lines. A refugee might cross a border, but remain within the same church. As such, while churches exist intentionally within national dynamics to serve their neighbours and contribute to the common good of society, their engagement can (and should) refrain from nation-state alignment. They exist not for a certain type of (national) people but to people as they are. In this way, churches are elastic to changes in the nation-state (and most certainly nation-states will come and go) but firm in a commitment to love people and places as they love themselves. Engaging in Christ's mission to any people in all places points to alternative ways of recognizing human dignity and demonstrating God's kingdom.

Summary

Forced displacement is one of the most pervasive forms of cruelty exerted on humans. It undermines humanity in all its forms and by corrupting a person's sense of place, purpose, and experience of belonging; though it is extremely familiar in the Middle Eastern context, it should never be seen as something normative or even inevitable. The chronic tragedy perpetuated upon forcibly displaced people must remind the Church that something is not right in the world, that the very systems organizing the world as we know it today are faulty. The plight of forcibly displaced people from, to, and within the region of the Middle East exposes a global modern crisis, while the response of churches illuminates how ecumenical cooperation in mission with and among the forcibly displaced can prophetically critique the rigid mechanisms of nation-states that perpetuate the crisis of forced displacement.

Mission and Discipleship in Context: A Contribution from Cyprus and the Gulf

John Holdsworth

The Context

The Anglican Diocese of Cyprus and the Gulf, as its name suggests, covers some ten political jurisdictions (depending on how you count) including all the countries of the Arabian/Persian Gulf. One of the striking elements of the context in which the Diocese pursues its mission is the massive growth in inward migration to the region. This migration is not, as so often seen nowadays, made up of refugees and economic migrants, but rather migration related to the economic growth of much of the area. The most obvious cause was the economic boom, particularly associated with the oil and gas extractive industries since the 1930s. Prior to that there had been some limited inward migration as a result of the geopolitical events which brought administrative officials from France and the UK, and which also established a military presence. The wealth generated by oil and gas exploration, particularly in the Arabian Gulf, attracted the other service industries associated with developed economies in the fields of law, education, retail and hospitality for example; and also those trades associated with massive construction projects. The result is, according to a UAE website, that over two hundred different nationalities live and work in the Emirates; and these migrants outnumber the indigenous population by a factor of at least 7:1. Many migrants come from Christian backgrounds, and it is no exaggeration to claim that, although they recognize themselves as guests, Christians vastly outnumber Muslims in the Gulf area. This is a new and unique mission situation. Of less importance but worthy of note is the temporary inward migration, as a result of tourism, made possible by increasing wealth in the "western" world, and relatively cheap and accessible means of travel. Whilst residence in the Gulf countries is only possible for those who are working there, Cyprus has become a retirement destination for people from northwestern Europe generally and Scandinavia and the UK in particular. There is also an appreciable Russian population in the island. This chapter will concentrate on the Gulf population, though some observations have relevance for Cyprus as well.

This Gulf population is transient, insecure (in the sense that their contracts may be terminated at short notice, requiring them to leave), of working age, and work-dominated (in the sense that they have little time or opportunity for anything else). Additionally, the migrant workers at the lower end of the economic scale are separated from their families, live in huge single sex accommodation, and have fewer participation rights or legal guarantees.

Throughout the countries of the Arabian Gulf, the Coptic, Latin Catholic, and Orthodox Churches are each represented, their buildings often forming a 'church city' on the outskirts of large towns. All attract large congregations of expats. In some jurisdictions, well-resourced Evangelical churches have separate buildings (as, for example in Abu Dhabi) but in the majority of cases, ethnic and other Protestant churches use facilities on the Anglican estate. The number of separate congregations using these facilities can number well over a hundred at the larger sites, and the Anglican church acts as their sponsor in the eyes of the various governments. This offering of what has come to be called 'hospitality' has a long history. As early as 1878, when Cyprus became, effectively, a British protectorate, and there were moves to "provide for the wants" of those English who might then settle there, it was made clear by the then appropriate bishop (actually the then bishop of Gibraltar) that "congregations under his remit would not be solely Anglicans, and therefore he welcomed those of non-conformist denominations as long as Anglican discipline was not undermined."[1]

One exception to this description is Iraq. Originally founded along the same lines as other British Colonial Anglican churches, more recently and especially since the invasion, the congregation at St George's Baghdad is largely indigenous, and worship is conducted in Arabic with some Aramaic. Mission takes a more traditional form there with the church providing clinic facilities, welfare provision, and a modern school, the School of the Redeemer, whose pupils are over 90 percent from a Muslim background. A similar story can be told with reference to the Anglican Church in the Yemen. When the British left Aden, the churches there closed, but subsequently Christ Church at Steamer Point reopened, not because of an expat demand but rather as the base for an eye clinic, which treats those local people, who could afford no other option. The clinic is staffed by, and ministers to a virtually exclusive Muslim population. Those who work there are more than happy to operate under 'a Christian flag.' The phrase one often hears in relation to that irony is "we are all people of the book." The clinic trains medical staff to assist the resident and temporary surgeons who offer their services there. In a country with 75 percent female illiteracy, such training offered is itself a creative contribution to society. The whole project deserves perhaps to be described as 'mission.' It has no ambition to recruit adherents to the Christian faith, but it does exemplify such faith in action.

The Chaplaincy Model

From the outset, the aim of the Anglican church was to provide for the spiritual needs of its own members, usually, though not exclusively, of its own (English) nationals. The earliest clergy to minister in the region were chaplains with a specific remit; either as military chaplains or seafarer chaplains. They were joined at a later date by industrial chaplains, paid for by employers. That particular model of ministry – the chaplaincy model – has dictated the structure of subsequent church life. This means that 'winning converts' has never been a primary mission ambition for the Church's work in the region. Indeed, great care was taken to declare that proselytism was not intended, and that respect for indigenous established Christian churches was to be maintained and developed.

[1] Angela Murray, *The Anglican Diocese of Cyprus and the Gulf: The unfolding Story* (London: Gilgamesh, 2020), 20, 22.

In the predominantly Muslim areas that same respect was to be observed. In 1970, at the beginning of what we might call the modern period, the then archdeacon in the Gulf set out relationships thus.

> Here, Christians far from home can maintain the continuity of their faith amidst a world that still worships faithfully in response to the call from the minaret. Each in their way can discover they have something to offer each other as they come to know each other better. Here where Western Christianity lives alongside Eastern Christianity and both live as guests in a Muslim world, all stand to gain from the faith of each other.[2]

This view underpins an ecclesiology that equates the Church with the embassy of a foreign country. It is to be a home from home. It will provide not only the assurance of things familiar, but will also provide a social space to meet other people with whom social relations may be creative. It will help to orientate newcomers and perhaps have some kind of welfare provision for members in need. In relation to the five marks of mission, it will give an authorized space in which to proclaim the gospel through preaching. It will give a structure to Christian nurture of children and adults alike, possibly through programmes leading to confirmation for example, or discipleship courses. It will offer pastoral support where necessary and encourage stewardship of God's creation. It will also be able to fulfil most of the challenges of the Arusha Call to Discipleship.[3]

However, there are limits to a chaplaincy model of ministry and mission. The mark of mission that calls on Christians to transform the unjust structures of society is not going to be easy to fulfil, for example. The Arusha Call to Discipleship challenge: "We are called to worship the one Triune God – the God of justice, love, and grace – at a time when many worship the false god of the market system (Luke 16:13),"[4] is also likely to conflict with social reality. And what preachers might want to say about conspicuous consumption and reverence for creation, in relation to the fifth mark of mission, might have to be shelved. The underlying problem is not confined to the Gulf region. It is a problem of the chaplaincy model wherever it is found. Chaplains are usually provided by institutions as part of the welfare provision for employees, in the belief that a workforce that feels it is cared for will be more effective or productive. Individual chaplains often find themselves caught between this aim and their own motivation. Is the military chaplain there to make better soldiers or to make better Christians? Is it the role of the chaplain to encourage the congregation to question the whole concept of military force, for example? The chaplaincy model is almost always a constrained model. It involves treating 'the congregation' as if it were a discreet institution in its own right; like a hospital community or a prison community, and that is at odds with the overriding ethos of Anglicanism

---

[2] Ibid., 128.

[3] The Arusha Call to Discipleship is a short statement with commitments that are relevant to Christian mission. The statement was issued during a conference on world mission and evangelism organized by the World Council of Churches in Tanzania in 2018.

[4] "The Arusha Call to Discipleship," www.oikoumene.org/resources/documents/the-arusha-call-to-discipleship.

as it developed in Britain, originally, and as it is still practiced there, as an open resource constrained only by geography – the so-called parish system. Anglican churches do not have membership lists (electoral rolls are rather different), and although the original establishment of the churches did define a discreet constituency, the current situation in the Gulf is far less clear.

The chaplaincy model is essentially responsive. It responds to the demands of its members. It is less likely to be proactive. This can mean that congregations adopt a customer mentality, and that clergy see themselves as service providers rather than something more dynamic. The chaplaincy model assumes transience, and so some features of settled churches, such as the encouragement of ministry vocations, can be ignored. The clergy themselves sometimes adopt the mindset of transience and so a chaplaincy can change ministers at a rapid rate and find that it is led over a short period by a bewildering variety of styles.

A further distinctive element of chaplaincy is that it tends to deal with individuals in isolation from their true lived context. A hospital or prison chaplain will deal with the patient or the prisoner as they find themselves outside their 'normal' family or community. This again does not fit easily with the church situation in the Gulf. True, those in the work camps have little agency over their own freedoms of movement and so, typically, the church goes to them by offering what is in effect a sector ministry within the wider ministry of the church. Until the Covid 19 pandemic, sector ministers were employed in Sharjah. In Al Ain the congregation developed a relationship with a women's camp that involved the congregation providing toiletries, sanitary products and other items on a regular basis. Visitors' groups have been set up in other places such as Jebel Ali. This replicates the relationship that a parish church might have with a local institution within its boundaries. And for the most part, ministry is indeed offered to families within what, for the time being, is normal life. So, the Anglican churches were set up on a chaplaincy understanding of ministry, and there are still clear expectations of that in some quarters. But, in fact in the Gulf they are also operating on a parish basis. This clearly calls for some reflection.

What do we mean by 'Church?'
The Ecclesiological Challenge 1: Diversity

To understand its ministerial theology within this special context, more clearly, in recent years the Diocese of Cyprus and the Gulf has sought to develop its own specific ecclesiology. Its most recent iteration of its Constitution allows the word 'parish' to be used alongside chaplaincy for example, to mitigate the sense of simply service providing and to explore more deeply what the five marks of mission might involve in this context. A vocational discernment process, together with a ministerial training programme has led to lay ministers being licensed and clergy being ordained, drawn from these expat congregations, and ministering to them. But at another level, this context for ministry invites theological thinking about ecclesiology and identity.

The conclusion of the Diocese of Cyprus and the Gulf is that a local ecclesiology, and hence a local statement of mission, inevitably begins with diversity. This is a core Biblical theme, with strong contemporary reference. The initial chapters of Genesis pose the fundamental question: is diversity a blessing or a curse? Is it God's intention or is it God's response to human sinfulness – hence a kind of punishment? In our contemporary world, should we consider diversity to be a threat, or should we embrace it as a means of truly understanding God's economy? The account of the tower of Babel in (the JE account of) Genesis 11:1-9 is often cited as an example of the latter, in contrast with the P account in chapter 10 which appears to regard the division of nations and languages as natural and unworthy of further comment (10:5). A different interpretation is suggested by the feminist liberation theologian Letty Russell. She believes that God sees the dangers for free society in a single dominant power backed up by a single language. She has in mind the situation in the US until recently in which a gradual extension of American soft power is backed up by military might, and the imposition of a single language (English) for all the important communications of power. On this reading the scattering of peoples and development of individual languages is a form of liberation from domination. The passage demonstrates that, "important ways of assuring that God's gift of riotous diversity in all creation will continue."[5] For Russell, diversity is an important theological axiom of creation. "God does not like uniformity in human life, in community or in nature;"[6] and, "God's intention is to create a world full of riotous difference."[7]

Also, on this reading Pentecost is an affirmation of Babel, rather than its reversal, as is often claimed. Luke's universalist (nowadays we might almost say globalist) view inevitably involves his seeing diversity as part of God's intention. His 'Pentecostalist model' rejoices in a unity within diversity view. When Luke describes the birth of Jesus as happening at a time and place where the 'whole world' is engaged in a common task, notably, the Greek word used for 'world' is not the geographical term, *kosmos*, but rather the socially descriptive word, *oekoumene*. He goes on to describe the birth of the church at Pentecost at a time when representatives of 'every nation under heaven' were present, with the familiar roll call of the Jewish diaspora. Russell's conclusion with regard to present church life is that "God expects a unity that is rooted in our recognition that the growing diversity of the church and the world is a gift of God, rather than a threat to our own comfortable life and faith."[8]

The church in the region has a unique opportunity to experience diversity and to respond to those Biblical perspectives. Even in Cyprus it is commonplace to have several ethnicities in the congregation, and in the Gulf, where there are many diaspora groups, diversity is the most striking feature of any service. If God chose to be born as a human and if he chose to launch his church and make his Spirit incarnate in the lives of his followers in a situation of diversity, this should count for something. If he were to be born today perhaps it would be in a shed in the back streets of Dubai! The diversity is not just ethnic, but in many

---

[5] Letty M. Russell, *Just Hospitality* (Louisville, KY: Westminster John Knox Press, 2009), 55.

[6] Ibid., 53.

[7] Ibid., 54.

[8] Ibid., 63.

places ecumenical, in the church sense of the word, in that the Anglican Church and the Latin Catholic Church are sometimes the only English-speaking mainline churches available to worshippers. However, it could be justly claimed that the diversity, though extensive, is not universal. This reflects Gulf society to an extent. Hence same-sex couples are not in evidence because they are effectively illegal. Disabled and very elderly frail are also not in evidence because third nation citizens are required to leave when they reach (a fairly low by modern standards) retirement age. For those who see this as a justice issue, there are considerable constraints in speaking out about it.

The Ecclesiological Challenge 2: Hospitality

The role of the Anglican Church in offering a home for those whose religious tradition has been formed in a Church not represented in the Gulf or in Cyprus, points to a feature of culture throughout the Middle East, namely open and generous hospitality. This operates at a number of levels. There is the gracious hospitality of the state authorities and indigenous religious bodies, which is offered to Christian churches generally. The UAE Minister for Tolerance is on record, speaking at St Andrew's Church in Abu Dhabi, as offering a huge tent under which all can shelter as they travel, so reintroducing a traditional metaphor. In biblical times, even in the desert phase, tents were pitched with the opening facing the direction that strangers might come from, so that they might be welcomed. The Orthodox Church of Cyprus offers a generous welcome to the Anglican Church there. Throughout the Middle East there is, among the Abrahamic religions, a shared sense of being 'people of the book' which, as we have noted above, is sometimes advanced.

Then there is the ecumenical hospitality, already mentioned, that sees the Anglican estate being used by other Christian denominations; and the willingness of the Anglican Church to act as their sponsor. Many of these Churches have an ethnic basis and there is something quite striking about walking through an Anglican campus on a worship day and seeing the incredible mixture of national dress and hearing the variety of languages. This is particularly true at Christmas when many of the churches are including nativity plays in their worship. Simply physically experiencing the variety of expressions of 'Christmas' is truly humbling, and it gives a whole new force to the idea of a post-colonial Anglican Church.

A third kind of hospitality is that experienced *within* the Anglican congregations. Here, people of many nationalities, colours, cultures, and classes embody hospitality toward each other. In recent years there has been a deal of writing about hospitality as a Christian axiom. Some writers have approached the subject through the prism of 'neighbour;'[9] others through the prism of 'stranger.'[10] Theological building blocks include the dynamics of the kingdom

---

[9] For example, Robert Carter and Samuel Wells, eds., *Who Is My Neighbour* (London: SPCK, 2018).

[10] For example, Arthur Sutherland, *I Was a Stranger: A Christian Theology of Hospitality* (Nashville: Abingdon Press, 2006).

(e.g., Matthew 25:34); a Christology based on Jesus' own experience of being a stranger (Matthew 8:20); the example of Abraham's hospitality in Genesis 18:3-5 (cf., Hebrews 13:2), and a response to the cross (Romans 12:13). Table fellowship is also cited, in the construction of these theologies, and of course that is related to Eucharist. The ongoing spiritual tradition of pilgrimage and the idea of a restless soul finding its welcome home, in Augustine's *Confessions*, is an important traditional theme.[11] All of which bears witness to the ubiquity and importance of hospitality as a theme in Christian thought.

Christ himself in fact could be said to have suffered all the deprivations listed in the parable of the sheep and the goats in Matthew 25. He too had been hungry, thirsty, and in his passion, both a prisoner and effectively naked. John's Gospel prologue describes how "his own received him not," the most obvious meaning of which is that they did not offer him hospitality (rather than the extrapolated "they did not recognise him as the Christ" though, this being John, both meanings are probably intended). Luke 7:44-47 describes how Jesus is 'received' by the unlikeliest of people, whilst the supposed host ignores the rules of hospitality. The Genesis 18 incident as recalled in Andrei Rublev's icon is sometimes taken as an expression of the Trinity. Nadim Nassar, who considers the Trinity to be, "the ultimate model of fellowship and relationships," believes that in his many interactions involving hospitality Jesus displays what he calls the culture of God. "He wants to teach us the very fact that his being with us, living in our culture, is an ultimate expression of the hospitality that God shows to humanity."[12] In the New Testament, very significant occasions are played out in the context of a meal, and in the story of Zacchaeus we see how hospitality is linked to salvation (Luke 19:5, 9). The Eucharist, in which Christ is in a sense both guest and host, gives opportunity for the congregation to be both host and guest.

There is a sense in which hospitality can itself be a catalyst of justice and transformation. This is reflected in Russell's definition of hospitality. "I suggest that hospitality is the practice of God's welcome by reaching out across difference to participate in God's actions bringing justice and healing in our world of crisis and our fear of the ones we call 'other'."[13] Throughout history, rootless people have usually been treated with anxiety. The suspicion surrounding the epithet of 'the wandering Jew,' for example, has been traced back to the seventh century,[14] providing an engine for antisemitism; and examples of hostility towards gypsies abound. In the New Testament, hospitality is theologically serious and linked with the justice theme of reconciliation. God welcomes those who are far off and makes them one through the reconciling work of the cross (Ephesians 2:11-14, cf. Romans 15:7). Jesus' action of foot washing is more than a gesture of servanthood. It is the accepted initial gesture of welcome. In the Gulf, where all people are in a sense rootless, an

---

[11] Augustine, *Confessions*, 1.1.2.

[12] Nadim Nassar, *The Culture of God* (London: Hodder and Stoughton, 2018), 13 and 48.

[13] *Russell, Just Hospitality*, 54.

[14] George Kumler Anderson, *The Legend of the Wandering Jew* (Providence RI: Brown University Press, 1965), 11.

unconditional hospitality can indeed be a marker for justice and an ambition for mission.

The Ecclesiological Challenge 3: Transience

Many of the congregants are resident aliens. 1 Peter in the NT is addressed to *paroikoi,* which, according to one writer, is a technical term for 'guest workers' appropriately translated as 'resident aliens.' "Denoting the 'stranger' or the 'alien' in a general way (this term) applied to persons who were differentiated from the natives among whom they lived in respect of their land of origin, ethnic or familial roots, their different views and opinions, and their language property and religion. In general, furthermore, such distinctions inevitably involved political, legal, economic and social restrictions and disadvantages for those so identified as strangers and foreigners."[15] This context has a direct relationship with discipleship for the author. These are people without power of any kind, and so all the exhortations in the Epistle are towards endurance, and the kinds of examples that can be set by people without power. Discipleship is evidenced by the response to (usually unjustified) suffering. (This status leads to a relatively unique discussion about how social responsibility is to be conducted when the Church does not have the ear of government, as it does for example in the UK and many other western governments).

The Diocese of Cyprus and the Gulf is probably the Diocese of the Anglican Communion which includes most expat members. We are used to hearing this term describe UK nationals living abroad, but in the context of the Diocese of Cyprus and the Gulf, expats from other countries hugely outnumber them. Some diaspora groups are catered for by churches of their particular ecclesial families, often coinciding with ethnic identities. There are expats at all levels of society. People who experience life outside their own birth country fall into several categories. Some are reluctant, and some willing, exiles. Some are working in the area for a while, some making it their long-term home (in Cyprus for example). Some are involved in marriages with people of a different nationality that has influenced where they live. Some engage with their context, whilst others do not. Some are pilgrim visitors, some are trippers. Some would self-identify as exiles. For the most part, the words of Jeremiah 29:4-7 are the ones that influence the ways Christians live:

> Thus says the LORD of hosts, the God of Israel, to all the exiles whom I have sent into exile from Jerusalem to Babylon: Build houses and live in them; plant gardens and eat what they produce. Take wives and have sons and daughters; take wives for your sons, and give your daughters in marriage, that they may bear sons and daughters; multiply there, and do not decrease. But seek the welfare of the city where I have sent you into exile, and pray to the LORD on its behalf, for in its welfare you will find your welfare.

Nevertheless, the loss of a former identity can be a problem for expats and exiles alike. Working, living and worshipping in new surroundings is always a

[15] John H Elliott, *A Home for the Homeless*, second edition (Eugene, OR: Wipf and Stock, 2005), 67.

challenge whether for a short period or as a long-term home. A Christian life in a new context with people coming from many different countries and traditions poses both difficulties and opportunities for both the individuals and ministry. A particular ministry of Anglican churches in the Gulf is the marriage ministry, for example. Marriage is certainly viewed by Gulf culture as being a cornerstone of settled society, and the church is often the best place to facilitate that. These issues are also important for the substantial diaspora communities of Churches indigenous to the Middle East.

Singing the songs of Zion is not always a sad or nostalgic thing. Inevitably, exiles want to be accepted as people with a culture and narrative and identity of their own that demands to be taken seriously and equal to local culture. In the Diocese of Cyprus and the Gulf, in our churches, there are also those who have a folk memory of colonial attempts to subdue local cultures, or to regard them as secondary to those of western Europe. This gives hospitality some of its importance, and gives even greater impetus for opportunities, for example, to worship in a mother tongue or with a particular cultural emphasis. In our Diocese, there is no such thing as 'when in Rome.' The Anglican churches in the Gulf, for example, offer worship in Arabic, Mandarin, Urdu, Igbo, Tamil and Marathi, as well as English.[16]

Comparing the role and self-understanding of the Anglican Church in this region with its self-understanding in, say, the UK, or indeed the context of many other churches within the Communion whose members often have not travelled far from their place of birth. can help to define its particularity. David Goodhart has drawn attention to the importance, for contemporary politics and the understanding of British society, of the distinction between those he calls Somewheres, and those he calls Anywheres. Somewheres are those whose identity is very much associated with a birthplace from which they have not travelled far. He notes that, "today, about three in five Britons still live within twenty miles of where they lived when age 14."[17] In the Gulf there are many thousands of labourers who would regard themselves as effectively forced to seek economic advantage away from their native land, and they may well identify as Somewheres, at best tolerating the conditions in which they live and dreaming of home and family. Most intentional professional expats, and retirees would identify as Anywheres; that is, "people who have portable 'achieved' identities, based on educational and career success, which makes them generally comfortable and confident with new places and people."[18] There is perhaps an interesting discussion to be had about ways of organising church based on this distinction, where, "the old distinctions of class and economic interest have not disappeared but are increasingly overlaid by a larger and looser one – between the people who see the world from Anywhere, and the people who see it from Somewhere."[19] Certainly, the predominant understanding and expression of church in many places, is essentially based and organized on ideas of settledness.

---

[16] Murray, *The Anglican Diocese of Cyprus and the Gulf*, 344-345.

[17] David Goodhart, *The Road to Somewhere* (London: Penguin Books, 2017), xv.

[18] Ibid., 3.

[19] Ibid., 3.

Church members in the Diocese, have experience of being sojourners and of the temporary and often precarious nature of their residence. Discipleship in this context involves considering the things that really bring security. As the Epistle to the Hebrews makes clear, we are all strangers and sojourners upon earth.[20] Church experience here means that we have a very real awareness of that.

It is fashionable in church circles to talk about occupying liminal space. Our working in places where boundaries are very evident and have to be negotiated with care gives this sometimes-whimsical concept a grounding in lived experience. In Cyprus there is the last divided capital city in Europe, with a green line patrolled by UN troops. In the Gulf jurisdictions, some are at war, and relations between others are politically taut. As a Church, for historic reasons, the Anglicans have very good relations with rulers and governments across the patch and have the privilege of modelling something important. There are churches on both sides of the green line in Cyprus, and there is a chaplaincy service to students at the biggest university on the island within the Muslim jurisdiction. Interfaith relations are excellent and based on mutual respect. This is not just an institutional characteristic. Church members habitually invite Muslim representatives to attend special services, which they do naturally and gladly. In some other parts of the world, these kinds of descriptions would seem incomprehensible. Discipleship here is partly defined by such experiences of courteous life together.

In an Anglican context where all too often the situation in England is taken as the norm and paradigm, it is perhaps as well to be reminded that the situation faced by the earliest church owes more to the situation in Abu Dhabi than the one in Amersham. In a wider perspective there is surely much to learn from those who, like Paul, spend some time in Arabia.

[20] Hebrews 11: 13-16.

Cooperation in Creation Care

Rima Nasrallah

The world is a work of art,
set before all for contemplation,
so that through it
the wisdom of Him who created should be known.

Basil of Caesarea[1]

At the beginning of September 2022, 220 young people from more than ten different Christian traditions in Lebanon walked together on a remote mountain path to encounter and pray for creation. This was the second year that the Middle East Council of Churches had called for the celebration of the Season of Creation. For the participating youth, this walk was both a breath of fresh air and a sobering reality. The event was received as a sign from the churches that they are concerned about: (i) climate change (ii) the present and future of young people and (iii) the intimate connection between ecological issues and spiritual issues. However, since the youth were also disheartened by the deplorable state of affairs in this region plagued by wars, economic crises, and political unrest, issues pertaining to the climate and environment had been pushed down the public priority list, as living conditions continued to deteriorate. The hike itself along a dried-up riverbed, in a thinning forest, and facing hideous quarries was a clear reminder of how quickly Lebanon was losing its biodiversity, natural resources, and beauty.

While the region as a whole is clearly suffering from the drastic ecological changes, many find it difficult to make a connection between ecology, faith, and spirituality. This chapter first sketches some of the ecological challenges and then proposes a few ways to frame creation care in a way that organically fits with eastern Christian spirituality. The chapter also highlights some initiatives where ecumenical action is already taking place in the region.

A Warming Region

"Humanity is on the brink of an abyss," proclaimed Metropolitan Mor Coorilos of the Syriac Orthodox Church in 2011.[2] Since then, scientists have identified nine "planetary boundaries" necessary for the stability and support of life as we know it, and all reports point to the fact that we have now stubbornly and

---

[1] Quoted in Oleh Kindiyeh, "Patrology, Ecology and Eschatology: Looking forward to the Future of the Planet by Looking Back to the Fathers of the Church," *Logos: A Journal of Eastern Christian Studies* 55:3–4 (2014), 303–327; quotation taken from page 316.

[2] Geevarghese Mor Coorilos, "Toward a Missiology That Begins with Creation," *International Review of Mission* 100:2 (2011), 310–321.

knowingly exceeded most of these boundaries.[3] By doing this we are destabilizing the climate, decreasing biodiversity, and polluting vital natural resources. In fact, we are only a few parts per million by volume of carbon dioxide away from the impossibility of life on this planet – some say we are moving towards a "mass extinction period."[4] Despite this bleak prospect, in most countries in the Middle East little if any attention is given to climate concerns.

Though the Middle East is warming at twice the global average,[5] climate problems are confounded and sometimes overshadowed by the protracted situation of war and mounting humanitarian needs making climate care seem a secondary if not a luxury issue.

Yet, there is no hiding from the realities of the region. Basra in Iraq has been flagged as one of the hottest points on earth competing only with Mitribah in Kuwait with temperatures increasing every year. The Jazeera area in northeast Syria has been suffering for years from dramatic droughts, jeopardizing the livelihoods of Syrians and Iraqis.[6] These changes in climate, with water scarcity and loss of agricultural land being the most detrimental, have caused dramatic demographic reconfigurations adding pressure on urban areas where groundwater tables are falling along with increased pollution and salinization.

Not only do most countries in the region share water sources across borders,[7] which leads to continuous diplomatic conflicts between neighbouring countries, this is also "the most water-short region in the world."[8] Desertification is sweeping across Iraq, Syria, Jordan, and Iran threatening the livelihood of millions. An increasing segment of the population in the area is suffering from

---

[3] Johan Rockström and Mattias Klumm, *Big World, Small Planet: Abundance within Planetary Boundaries* (New Haven and London: Yale University Press, 2015).

[4] Mary Evelyn Tucker and John Grim, "The Movement of Religion and Ecology: Emerging field and dynamic force," in *The Routledge Handbook of Religion and Ecology*, ed. Willis Jenkins, Mary Evelyn Tucker and John Grim (London and New York: Routledge, 2017), 6.

[5] Kenzie Azmi, "Middle East and North Africa faces extreme climate change threat," *Greenpeace*, 2 November 2022, https://www.greenpeace.org/international/story/56469/middle-east-north-africa-mena-faces-extreme-climate-change-threat/, accessed 3 December 2022.

[6] This has been going on since 2006 after a multiyear drought hit Syria. On the link between climate change, violence and extremism in Syria and Iraq, see: Jamal Saghir, "Climate Change and Conflicts in the Middle East and North Africa" (Report published by the Issam Fares Institute for Public Policies and International Affairs at the American University of Beirut, 2019).

[7] Syria and Iraq depend on the Tigris and Euphrates rivers, which rise from southeastern Turkey. Iraq shares water with Iran. Egypt shares the Nile with 11 countries. Jordan's two main surface water resources, the Jordan and Yarmouk rivers, are shared with its neighbours. Lebanon and Syria share the Assi river. Kuwait and Bahrain's groundwater reserves are fed by water flowing underground from Saudi Arabia.

[8] Roberto L. Lenton, "Introduction," in *Water Security in the Middle East: Essays in Scientific and Social Cooperation*, ed. Jean Axelrad Cahan (London, New York, Melbourne, Delhi: Anthem Press, 2017), xi.

water and food insecurity. A recent cholera outbreak in Lebanon and Syria was, according to a UNICEF report, "threatening children's survival."[9]

All these changes have "significant political, environmental, social and economic implications."[10] Some analysts believe that climate change is one of the contributing factors to many of the regional wars, particularly in Syria and Iraq. Loss of good farming land drove many despairing young people to join extremist groups who promised them alternative economic solutions. This situation adds to the increasing impoverishment and deteriorating health of the population.

It is therefore astounding that local governments hardly pay any attention to climate change, even when COP27 took place in Sharm el Sheikh, Egypt, and COP28 is scheduled to take place in Dubai in December 2023. Civil society's initiatives also remain shy and sporadic.

Shifting the Blame

To many in the Middle East, climate change seems to be both caused by the West and then proposed as an agenda item by the same West or developed countries. During COP26 in Glasgow, Indian activist Vijay Prashard lashed out at the West accusing its "permanent colonialism" of being the root cause of problems in the global South and pointing to the fact that "our children are not worried about the future, they are worried about their present."[11] Similar sentiments can be heard in the Middle East.

A number of theologians also point to Western economic, ideological, and even theological systems as a source of environmental degradation. Blaming the West for what Archbishop Rowan Williams declared in 2014 as its "destructive western lifestyle"[12] as well as for its system of reasoning and theological discourse has become commonplace. The theological discourse often critiqued is a product of a marriage between modernity and Christianity, particularly in its Western form, which has tainted our understanding of the world, shifted our self-perception as human beings and corrupted our cosmologies. John Chryssavgis, Archdeacon to the Ecumenical Patriarchate, points out that "Western thought in the modern age" in particular "has not been kind to the created world."[13] Chryssaygis points out that René Descartes saw humans as the only rational

---

[9] Bertrand Bainvel, "Cholera outbreaks threaten children's survival in the Middle East," *UNICEF*, 24 October 2022, https://www.unicef.org/press-releases/cholera-outbreaks-threaten-childrens-survival-middle-east, accessed 3 December 2022.

[10] Lenton, "Introduction," xi.

[11] Vijay Prashard People's Summit Speech from OUR TIME IS NOW#3, accessed 3 December 2022, https://www.youtube.com/watch?v=Bho6xY-jSuE.

[12] "Former Archbishop of Canterbury reveals global climate change fears," *The Guardian*, 30 March 2014, accessed 3 December 2022, https://www.theguardian.com/uk-news/2014/mar/30/archbishop-canterbury-rowan-williams-climate-change-fears.

[13] John Chryssavgis and Bruce V. Foltz, *Toward an Ecology of Transfiguration: Orthodox Christian Perspectives on Environment, Nature and Creation* (New York: Fordham University Press, 2013), 2.

beings, wholly separate from and superior to nature and animals which he perceived as mere mindless instruments to be mastered and exploited at will. Chryssaygis further shows that Hegel approached the natural world as a spirit in a degraded and paralyzed condition and that there were numerous others who perceived the world, in the words of Max Weber, as a "disenchanted" entity, unable to elicit in us any wonder or sense of transcendence.[14]

Unfortunately, there is an amalgam of Christianity and Western thought[15] that has backfired and led some, such as American historian Lynn White Jr,[16] to accuse Christianity of being singularly responsible for the present environmental crisis.[17] Admittedly, a major strand of Christianity – in the West as well as the East – has tended to interpret the world in anthropocentric terms. It has viewed the material world as primarily for human use and set humans above creation, and distinct from it. Humans were considered to be in a position to master it, based on a God-given sanction such as the one interpreted in the book of Genesis. Such ways of thinking have helped usher in the age of the Anthropocene.[18]

In addition, some within Christianity have interpreted salvation history as primarily concerning human beings.[19] They have framed salvation as a liberation from the created material order into a heavenly spiritual realm.[20] Even more, certain understandings of salvation look forward to the final destruction of this world.[21]

Add to this the blame that Max Weber – in his often-cited thesis – directs towards Protestantism connecting it with a spirit of diligent work and accumulation of wealth,[22] facilitating eventually the rise of global capitalism and with it the growth of consumerist ideologies. These in turn have led to greater divides between rich and poor and have exhausted nature.[23] Though the direct connection between Protestantism and capitalism remains debatable,[24] we have witnessed how "nature has been reduced to measurable entities for profit or use"

---

[14] Ibid.

[15] Whether this amalgam started with Hellenic philosophy, Augustine or Modern assumptions about the world is beyond the scope of this paper.

[16] Lynn White Jr, "The Historical Roots of Our Ecological Crisis," *Science* 155:3767 (1967), 1203-1207.

[17] This is a misunderstanding or exaggeration collapsing a modern view of the world developed in the 17th and 18th century into an all-Christian attitude.

[18] For more on the Anthropocene, see Clive Pearson, "Acting Justly in the Anthropocene: Considering the Case for a Christian Social Ethics," *Enacting a Public Theology*, ed. Clive Pearson (Stellenbosch: SUN MEDIA, 2019), 87-98.

[19] Daniel L. Migliore, *Faith Seeking Understanding: An Introduction to Christian Theology* (Grand Rapids: Eerdmans, 1991), 80.

[20] Ernst M. Conradie and Hilda P. Koster, *Christian theology and Climate Change in the North Atlantic Context* (Edinburgh: T&T Clark, 2020).

[21] Hal Lindsey, *The Late Great Planet Earth* (Grand Rapids: Zondervan, 1970).

[22] Max Weber, *The Protestant Ethic and the Spirit of Capitalism*, trans. Talcott Parsons (London and New York: Routledge, 2001, first ed. 1930).

[23] Unlike what Adam Smith projected in his book *The Wealth of Nations* (1776).

[24] Michael S Northcott, "Reformed Protestantism and the Origins of Modern Environmentalism," *Philosophia Reformata* 83:1 (2018), 19–33.

and how we have come to "imagine and implement a utilitarian-based worldview."[25]

However, blaming Christianity as a religion or blaming Western thought alone for the ecological crisis is neither fair nor helpful. It can only create dichotomies and exempt some from their responsibility. Ernst M. Conradie's proposal of a four-task Christian ecology is probably most helpful here. In his treatment of the subject he calls for "an ecological critique of Christianity and a Christian critique of ecological destruction, a constructive contribution to Christian authenticity and on that basis to multi-disciplinary discourse on ecological concerns in the public sphere."[26] While acknowledging the role that the Christian tradition and certain discourses within it have played in ecological damage, we are also thankful that church leaders and ecumenical bodies have been avant garde and most vocal in advocacy and call for change.

Calling for Creation Care

We have heard these calls in documents such as the World Council of Churches (WCC) programme on *Justice, Peace and the Integrity of Creation*, starting at the Vancouver assembly in 1983, and then, following a Europe-wide meeting in Basel in 1989, reaching its climax in Seoul in 1990. The WCC also issued a "Call to Climate Action" during the Copenhagen negotiations in 2009. The climate work of the WCC continued and found a recent expression in the statement "The Living Planet: Seeking a Just and Sustainable Global Community," which was issued by the WCC's 11th Assembly in Karlsruhe, Germany, in 2022. The ACT Alliance and the WCC have begun using the term *ecodiakonia* to emphasize the close connection between two areas of priority: service and creation care.[27]

Among churches, we have heard the calls from Greek Orthodox theologians such as the previous Ecumenical Patriarch Demitrios I, who, in 1989, designated September 1 as 'the World Day of Creation,' and his successor Patriarch Batholomew I, rightly called the green Patriarch. The Ecumenical Patriarchate considered "our relationship toward the natural environment" an "urgent concern and spiritual priority".[28] It supported research and encouraged Orthodox worldwide to care for God's creation. We have seen it in the works of Syriac theologians such as the Indian Metropolitan Geevarghese Mor Coorilos who anchors missiology in creation and sees mission as a reversal of humanity's destructive and dominating actions.[29] We have witnessed a growing concern for creation within the Anglican Communion, which led to the identification of

---

[25] Tucker and Grim, "The Movement of Religion and Ecology," 4.

[26] Ernst M. Conradie, "The Four Tasks of Christian Ecotheology: Revisiting the Current," *Scriptura* 119:1 (2020), 1-13. See also Ernst M. Conradie, *Christianity and Ecological Theology: Resources for Further Research* (Stellenbosch: SUN Press, 2006).

[27] Daniel Beros et al eds., *International Handbook on Creation Care and Eco-Diakonia* (Oxford: Regnum Books, 2022).

[28] Reference: Chryssavgis and Foltz, *Toward an Ecology of Transfiguration*, xi.

[29] Geevarghese Mor Coorilos, "Toward a Missiology That Begins with Creation," *International Review of Mission* 100:2 (2011), 310–321.

creation care as the fifth mark of mission.[30] Archbishops Rowan Williams and Justin Welby have pushed creation care higher up the Anglican agenda in various Lambeth statements and declarations. Finally, we have seen the effect of Pope Francis' encyclical *Laudato Si'*, which inspired a worldwide movement and influenced the Paris Agreement.[31]

Both individually and collectively, these leaders have spoken emphatically. In a joint statement issued in 2021, Pope Francis, Archbishop Justin Welby, and Patriarch Batholomew I reaffirmed the ecumenical imperative for "every Christian, believer and people of goodwill to play a part in changing our collective response to the threat of climate change and environmental degradation."[32] Together they reaffirmed that sin not only harms human beings but is also "degrading the integrity of the earth." They called for repentance and a drastic change in Christian thought, attitude, and behaviour. As they pointed out, this requires "an ever-closer collaboration among all churches in their commitment to care for creation."[33]

With these global calls in mind, we turn to the Middle East to see how and where Eastern Christian traditions and spirituality can contribute to an indigenous framing of ecological concerns and perhaps also inspire others. By doing this we do not intend to exempt Eastern forms of Christianity from their responsibility but rather focus on helpful aspects.

A Middle Eastern Christian Perspective

A number of Christian scholars in the Middle East have revisited their traditions to find inspiration and connections with climate concerns. This task is made easier as the East has not been as affected intellectually and spiritually by modernity and the Enlightenment and it has preserved in its cosmology a level of harmony within the created order. For both the Eastern and the Oriental churches the material world in particular and its symbolism play a major part in spirituality.[34] The wisdom of the Church Fathers, the richness of the liturgical-ritual, ascetic lifestyles, and the sacramental theology in the diverse traditions provide Eastern and Oriental Christians with powerful incentives to connect with creation.

---

30 https://www.churchofengland.org/sites/default/files/2021-05/CCB_Lambeth-declaration-2015-on-climate-change-updated.pdf accessed 25 January 2024.

31 https://www.vatican.va/content/francesco/en/encyclicals/documents/papa-francesco_20150524_enciclica-laudato-si.html, accessed 25 January 2024.

32 Benedict Mayaki, SJ, "Pope and ecumenical leaders: Caring for God's creation requires commitment", *Vatican News*, 7 September 2021, accessed 4 December 202, https://www.vaticannews.va/en/pope/news/2021-09/pope-bartholomew-justin-welby-creation-sustainability-message.html.

33 Ibid.

34 The term 'Eastern Churches' refers to the Orthodox churches who accept the Council of Chalcedon and the term 'Oriental Churches' to those who reject it.

Church Fathers and Creation

Within Eastern and Oriental Christian traditions, the church fathers wield significant authority in matters of doctrine, exerting profound influence on the perspectives shaping our understanding of creation. Patristic literature "provide(s) a cluster of biblical interpretations of the relationship between God and humanity, God and the environment, humanity and the environment, in very close interconnection and synergy."[35] Refuting Gnosticism and Neoplatonism, the fathers defended the goodness of creation proclaiming God as its creator and saviour. John Chrysostom, for example, emphasized the "ontological goodness of the created world" and cautioned against a "utilitarian" approach to creation.[36] The aesthetic dimension of creation was brought forth by Basil of Caesarea, who found value in the beauty of creation, declaring it "a work of art, set before all for contemplation, so that through it the wisdom of Him who created it should be known."[37] And Pseudo- Dionysius the Areopagite "explains the cohesive functioning of all creatures due to God's unifying love."[38] Moreover, the Fathers perceived the world in a sacramental manner, and they considered other creatures as partners in the praise of God. Many Fathers wrote prayers for creation, animate and inanimate, that have survived to this day and are used in liturgies, such as the prayers for animals by St Modestos and Saint Mamas.[39]

Liturgy (Common Prayer) and Rituals

Part of the world view in the Christian East is shaped by the liturgy (or common prayer) which is perceived as a cosmic liturgy, where the whole of creation participates in praise; things seen and unseen, human and non-human, on earth and in heaven. Through the language and music of the liturgy as well as the architecture and iconography, human beings are made aware that they participate in the liturgy alongside others in creation.

His Holiness Catholicos Aram I of the Armenian Apostolic Church asserts that the "Armenian spirituality is eco-centred; all aspects and elements of creation are harmoniously integrated to all the forms of practices, and expressions of spirituality."[40] Similarly, the Coptic liturgy prides itself in the rich ecological language of its prayers. In his article "Liturgy as Ethicizer," Stephen Meawad goes into the details of Coptic prayers, particularly the Midnight Praise, to show the extensive ecological references throughout the various forms of liturgical prayers. Meawad shows how not only the language but also the frequency of these prayers "work to transform those who recite them" and that

---

[35] Kindiyeh, "Patrology, Ecology and Eschatology, 313.
[36] Ibid., 316.
[37] Ibid., 317.
[38] Ibid.
[39] Some of their prayers can be found on:
http://panorthodoxconcernforanimals.org/prayers-for-creation/.
[40] Aram I, *The Armenian Church* (Antelias: Armenian Catholicosate of Cilicia, 2016), 139.

"one of the avenues of transformation is ecological awareness."[41] All this is illustrated in the Coptic Litany of fruits, plants and water:

> Pray for the air of heaven, the fruits of the earth, the rising of the waters of the rivers, the seeds, the herbs, and the plants of the field, that Christ our God may bless them, have compassion on His creation which His Hands have made, and forgive us our sins.[42]

We see similar patterns in the Greek Orthodox liturgy whose vespers start with Psalm 104, praising God for all of creation and offering it back to God in thanksgiving. Bishop Kallistos Ware points to "the Orthodox book of blessings and intercessions known in Greek as the Ευχολόγιον ('Book of Prayer') where "there are prayers for the good health of sheep, goats, and cattle, of horses, donkeys, and mules, and even of bees and silkworms."[43]

In general, Greek Orthodox theology understands humans as priests of creation, planted in it "not to exploit the created world after our own designs but rather to celebrate and consecrate and offer it back to the Creator."[44] This is reflected in the words of the Divine Liturgy- "Thine own of Thine own we offer unto Thee on behalf of all and for all." It is an affirmation that the whole cosmos originates in God and returns to the Creator including human beings and all their belongings.[45] This broad cosmic worldview is what enables us to imagine a world that is different from the one we have 'created' or become accustomed to. It is the conviction that something which has not yet happened can actually happen with everyone's cooperation and the synergy of God.[46]

The theology of the liturgy, its language and frequency are imbued with ecological themes, and this is expressed materially in the rituals and elements of nature that take centre stage in the various sacraments and the rhythm of the liturgical year. Besides the generous immersing in water at baptism and its blessing and spraying at Epiphany (Megas Agiasmos), some, such as the Armenians, celebrate transfiguration with a drenching water feast called Vardavar and the Cypriots celebrate Kataklysmos at Pentecost by the waterfront. Oriental traditions also include chrism (holy myron) in their sacraments. In the Coptic, Syriac and Armenian traditions, the chrism is a combination of more than forty natural elements: various flowers, plants and herbs – such as balsam,

---

[41] Meawad, Stephen, "Liturgy as Ethicizer: Cultivating Ecological Consciousness through a Coptic Orthodox Liturgical Ethos," in *T&T Clark Handbook of Christian Theology and the Modern Sciences*, ed. John P Slattery (Edinburgh: T&T Clark, 2020), 307-317, quotation taken from page 311.

[42] Deacon Responses: Litany of the Fruits, Water, Plants, *Tasbeha*, accessed 4 December 2022, https://tasbeha.org/hymn_library/view/1921.

[43] Kallistos Ware, "An Integrated Theology: Compassion for Animals," *Climate Crisis and Creation Care: Historical Perspectives Ecological Integrity and Justice*, ed. Christina Nellist (Newcastle, Barcelona, Berlin, Beijing: Cambridge Scholar Publishing, 2021), 8.

[44] Chryssavgis and Foltz, *Toward an Ecology of Transfiguration*, 4.

[45] Pseudo-Dionysius: *The Complete Works*, trans. Colm Luibheid (Mahwah, NJ: Paulist Press, 1987), 47-132.

[46] Patriarch Bartholomew, Climate Change: An Ecumenical Imperative, Address held at the University of Notre Dame, 28 October 2021.

cloves, ginger, cardamom, gum, sandal, saffron, cypress oil of rose, violet, myrtle leaves, and aloe – go into its making, thus using a variety of natural elements in the sacrament.[47] One can also point to the fact that feasts may be accompanied by the blessing of natural elements such as grapes or flowers at the Assumption of Mary, eggs at Easter, bread, wheat, wine and oil (Artoklasia) during vesper services, and a great number of other elements on different occasions. Not only are elements such as salt, water and dough blessed in the church but also in the homes of the faithful.

This understanding that God is present in his creation, through the Logos "cultivates a feeling of sacred, holy matter especially in the sacraments. The sacramental life is a restoration of creation, the medium for the experience of God."[48]

Asceticism and Monasticism

Another dimension of Eastern and Oriental spirituality in connection with ecological sensitivity is monasticism, the backbone of Christianity in the Middle East. All denominations declare that monasticism is a vital element of Christian spirituality and life, as evidenced by the Coptic desert monasticism of Saint Anthony and the Maronite monks of the Qadisha (holy) valley. We can learn a lot from the ascetic interaction with nature. Monasticism is not, as one assumes, a thing of the past. On the contrary it has experienced a great revival in the past century across the region and inspires young people and the community at large.[49] Monasticism expresses itself in a mode of being, in an attitude, and in a lifestyle.

The mode of being is, in the words of John Chryssavgis, "inaction" and "being" rather than "doing."[50] Eastern and Oriental monasticism are often perceived to be more contemplative than Western monasticism and therefore leading a life that produces less waste and leaves lighter footprints. Reflecting on the relation between ecology and monasticism, Archimandrite Vasileios says: "As a monk, you feel *at rest* because, what do you do? In that place, in that monastery, you dwell, you live and understand that there is a single essence and purpose for both the soul and the body."[51]

The attitude of monastic life is one of *kenosis* (self- emptying), a mode of existence seen in Christ's example, as described by the Apostle Paul in Philippians 2:7.[52] It is a countercultural way of life where, instead of

---

[47] Aram I, *The Armenian Church,* 126.

[48] Daniel Munteanu, "Cosmic Liturgy: The Theological Dignity of Creation as a Basis of an Orthodox Ecotheology," *International Journal of Public Theology* 4:3 (2010), 332-344, citation from page 336.

[49] See the chapter on monasticism and mission by Antoine Al Ahmar and Garen Yosolkanian in this volume.

[50] John Chryssavgis, "A New Heaven and a New Earth: Orthodox Theology and an Ecological World View," Ecumenical *Review* 62:2 (2010), 219.

[51] Chryssavgis, *Toward an Ecology of Transfiguration,* 351.

[52] Mor Coorilos, "Towards a Missiology that Begins with Creation," 310-321.

accumulating and amassing, one lets go. It is living "as having nothing yet possessing all things" (2 Cor. 6:10).

Finally, the ascetic lifestyle is one of renunciation, repentance and responsibility. John Chryssavgis sees in those three a close connection to ecological responsibility. He argues that renunciation leads to a lifestyle of simplicity. Repentance reminds us that we have fallen short of fulfilling our vocation to serve and preserve the earth and should "be prepared to reverse our perspectives and practices."[53] And responsibility leads us to focus our attention on glorifying God.

Fasting and Abstinence

Closely linked to monasticism but not restricted to it is the practice of fasting. In the Middle East, fasting is a public and communal activity. From billboard advertisements to changes in the menus of restaurants one can hardly miss the great fasting seasons. In Orthodox traditions fasting implies abstaining from foods containing meat, fats, milk and eggs. In other words, it means temporarily switching to a vegan diet. Though these are ancient traditions that precede the popularity of the term 'vegan,' today there is a greater awareness of the value of such fasting in relation to the environment and kindness toward animals.

Fasting periods are quite prolonged in the East. The Armenian liturgical calendar includes 160 days of fasting.[54] The Greek Orthodox have between 180 and 200 days. The Coptic Orthodox has up to 210 days. The faithful of the various churches fast during Advent, before Epiphany, during Lent, on Wednesdays and Fridays, and preceding the feast of the Assumption/Dormition of Mary. Some also observe the fast of the Ninevites (Assyrians, Copts and Ethiopians), and the fast of the Apostles.

A contemporary interpretation of patristic teachings on fasting, such as those of Maximus the Confessor and Origen of Alexandria, leads us to a perception of fasting as not only a "dietary restriction" but "consuming less energy" and "using fewer material goods."[55] Fasting is a reversal of gluttony, which was labelled as selfishness by Saint Gregory of Nyssa.[56] This greed is obvious in the way the world today produces, packages, markets, and transports food around the globe, causing soil and water pollution and the loss of habitats and biodiversity.

This manner of fasting challenges negative attitudes toward animals as merely a resource for humans and celebrates the friendship between humans and animals. The writings on asceticism by the 7th century Syriac bishop Isaac the Syrian include reflections on this human-animal friendship.[57]

---

[53] Nellist, *Climate Crisis*, 12.

[54] Aram I, *The Armenian Church*, 103.

[55] Oleh, "Patrology, Ecology and Eschatology," 320.

[56] Susan Holman, The *Hungry Are Dying: Beggars and Bishops in Roman Cappadocia* (Oxford: Oxford University Press, 2001), 198.

[57] Saint Isaac the Syrian, Homily 82, in *Mystic Treatises by Isaac of Nineveh*, tr. A. J. Wensinck, Amsterdam: Koninklijke Akademie van Wetenschappen, 1923.

The Land as Holy

It goes without saying that the Christians of this region regard the land as holy-from Egypt and its Nile to the Red Sea where a pivotal episode of salvation history played out; from Jerusalem and Bethlehem to the river Jordan where Jesus was baptized; from Tyre and Sidon, where the Lord walked, to the Straight Street in Damascus, where Paul was converted and finally to Antioch, where the followers of the Way were first called Christians: the land, its water, and landscape are witnesses to God's creative, salvific and providential work. In addition, each tradition has its particular attention to the land. We see this most clearly in the teachings of the Maronite Church in its Synod proceeding in 2006.

> With the Divine Incarnation, the land gained a value of salvation; thus, we should take care of it, preserve it, and respect it because it is no more a land belonging to Man alone but it has become the land of the Divine Incarnation. This theological understanding and concept of the land is carved in the Maronite spirit and that is what we look for in our liturgical prayers and in the writings of our blessed fathers.[58]

When combined with the theological and ritual-liturgical inspiration and the ascetic practices described above, the view of the land as holy can potentially translate into great blessings on the ground, as together the Maronite and the Orthodox Church of Antioch are "the largest owners of land in both Lebanon and Syria."[59]

Streams in the Desert

Despite the fact that Middle Eastern governments are not as engaged in the protection of creation and the environment as they should be, this theme is slowly gaining momentum among churches, youth movements, and faith-based NGOs. The following sample of initiatives illustrates this.

A Rocha Lebanon, is an evangelical organization for nature conservation with an ecumenical approach. It has worked in Lebanon since the 1990s to restore wetlands, secure safe passage for migrating birds, and to map biodiversity. In Palestine, the Evangelical Lutheran Church in Jordan and the Holy Land (ELCJHL) runs the Environmental Education Center (EEC), an educational ministry promoting a holistic awareness for all. In Jordan, the Episcopal Church in Jerusalem and the Middle East was at the forefront of rainwater harvesting initiatives. In Egypt, the Anafora Coptic community and retreat centre offers an alternative mode of being in harmony with creation. Some monasteries across the region offer spaces for young people to participate in traditional agricultural and organic practices. Inspired by *Laudato Si'*, a group of Maronite monks in the Mar Nohra monastery in Lebanon initiated, in 2021, an energy efficiency project to help both the locals and the environment. In 2019, the Holy Synod of Antioch, presided over by Patriarch John X, called the clergy to preach about the

---

[58] *Maronite Synod Proceedings* (Bkerke, 2006), 23.17 (p. 859).

[59] Bassam Nassif, "The Church of Antioch: Creation and Environmental Sustainability," *Climate Crisis and Creation Care,* 280.

sacredness of God's creation and to hold educational sessions in parochial schools, youth organizations, diocesan high schools, and the University of Balamand. It also issued the following statement about ecological concerns and the deteriorating environmental crisis:

> The Holy Synod calls for courageous living options that respect the environment and reduce the greed of consumption that dominate nature for quick and easy profit. The Synod also asks the governments to enforce policies that guarantee the prospects for future life and contribute to protecting the access by future generations to the goods of the earth.[60]

These and various initiatives, spanning from the Association of Catholic Patriarchs and Bishops to local youth movements and individual parishes, have surfaced in diverse levels and scopes. They inspire many to see their Christian mission intertwined with care for creation.

Yet cooperation between the various churches in this field began mostly when the Middle East Council of Churches (MECC) took up the task of organizing the Season of Creation from 2020. Churches across the Middle East and from all the ecumenical traditions started worshipping and celebrating together between 1 September and 4 October using the international manual for the Season of Creation, translated into Arabic and promoted by the MECC. Youth events were organized in a number of areas across the region. Youth groups, movements, and scouts undertook ecological activities such as cleaning beaches, planting trees, fishing plastic from rivers, and most importantly praying together and reaching out to the wider community.

As this is a novel topic from a theological perspective, the MECC in cooperation with the Association of Theological Institutes in the Middle East organized a symposium on eco-theology under the title, 'Ecumenical Perspectives on Climate Change' in October 2023. The symposium involved theologians from various traditions and scientists as well as faith-based organizations and activists. They shared and learned from each other and worked together to effect transformation of minds and change on the ground. In addition, churches and faith-based organizations have worked together for a wider representation and involvement in COP27 and COP28. All this shows that a new wind may be blowing.

Conclusion

In the movie "Costa Brava" (2021), writer and director Mounia Akl tells the story of a family who decided to leave the toxic pollution of Beirut and build a simple and organic life in the mountains. Little did its members know that their little paradise would soon be invaded by a garbage dump and lethal toxins ruining their health, and destroying their relationships and their mental health. This fictional drama shows that individual efforts and small initiatives are not enough to escape or combat the effects of ecological degradation and climate change. It

---

[60] Statement issued by the Holy Synod of Antioch, Balamand, 10 October 2019, accessed 25 July 2023, https://www.antiochpatriarchate.org/en/page/statement-issued-by-the-holy-synod-of-antioch-balamand-october-10-2019/2279/.

also shows that everything in society is endangered if harmony with creation is not sought.

In a region where political interests, sectarian and financial gains play a great role, it is time to see the larger picture and focus on how religion can be a solution rather than a tool used by some to cause division and violence. As we have seen, the churches have rich resources at their disposal that can help transform attitudes and actions: their theological ancestors, their liturgies and rituals, their ascetic practices, and indeed their relationship with the land itself. We have also seen how ecumenical efforts help sensitize the churches and how faith-based organizations and monasteries are holding up examples of care and restoration of nature. We pray that the little 'streams' of ecological care started by churches and Christian groups will unite and become a watershed of renewal in the region.

> "The earth is the LORD'S, and all that is in it, the world, and those who live in it."
>
> (Ps 24:1)

Mission: A Proclamation in Dialogue. A Focus on the Middle East Ecumenical Contribution to Interfaith Dialogue

Elias El Halabi

Introduction

This contribution surveys early encounters between people of different faiths that were sponsored by the World Council of Churches (WCC) during the second half of the 20th century. These early meetings were of great significance in establishing the foundations of interfaith dialogue. The chapter pays special attention to the pioneering roles of Middle Eastern Christian theologians and Muslim scholars as well as to the regional ecumenical bodies, mainly the Middle East Council of Churches (MECC). Lebanon with its multi-confessional identity provided an excellent venue to host these meetings. The chapter argues that these meetings played a crucial role in fostering mutual understanding between people of different faiths and instituting Christian-Muslim dialogue. A sketch of the historical development of the dialogues shows that, while the concept of interfaith dialogue was contested in missionary circles in the first half of the 20th century, the ecumenical movement provided an impetus for interfaith dialogue as a tangible expression of faith commitment and the freedom to proclaim one's religion in a pluralistic world, thus overcoming the dichotomy between witness and dialogue. This chapter relies on reports and statements that were issued by the various ecumenical dialogue meetings.

Christian-Muslim Relations in Ecumenical Discourse in the First Half of the 20th Century

A quick survey of the history of the ecumenical movement shows that the relation between Christianity and the other faiths was on the agenda from the very outset. The World Missionary Conference, which was held at Edinburgh in 1910, is regarded as a first milestone on the road of the modern ecumenical movement. This coming together of more than 1200 missionaries, mission secretaries and scholars, connected to a large number of missionary societies aiming at the evangelization of the world, faced the central issue of the understanding of and the relationship to other religious traditions.[1] In preparation for the conference elaborate questionnaires were sent out to missionaries worldwide. Specialized commissions were created to reflect on the eight focal areas of the conference. The report of commission IV titled: "The Missionary

[1] Guli E. Francis-Dehqani, "Adventures in Christian-Muslim Encounters since 1910," in *Edinburgh 2010: Mission Then and Now*, eds. David A. Kerr and Kenneth R. Ross (Oxford: Regnum Books and Carlisle: Paternoster Press, 2009), 125-138.

Message in relation to non-Christian Religions," was faced with the task of examining the obstacles to missionary work in a non-Christian world and how to make the gospel appealing to a non-Christian mind.[2] In order to better ponder on the abstract of replies to the questionnaire on this particular subject, five sub-committees were created to deal with the five fields of Animistic Religions, Chinese Religions, Japanese Religions, Islam, and Hinduism.[3] Here we focus on the deliberations related to Islam in particular.

The report of the sub-committee began with a historical and theological overview of Islam with all its offshoots. It gave a panoramic view, from a missionary perspective, of the different nuances of Islamic faith and practices in different Arab and Muslim countries. The quest for atonement and admiration of the Christian morality were seen as areas of great potential for missionary endeavours. Christianity was associated with progress, education and political superiority, while Islam was relegated to backwardness, ignorance and political humiliation.[4] The missionaries were polarized around two main attitudes: the affirmation of the uniqueness of Christianity as an embodiment of the full truth and the sympathy towards other religions viewed as imperfect revelations of this truth. At the conference, Pastor Gottfried Simon, a German missionary based in Sumatra, placed Islam in a middle position by affirming that "it has taken over several truths of Christianity, even if in a defective form."[5] Rev. Henry Harris Jessup, a Presbyterian missionary based in Lebanon, wanted to capitalize on the commonalities "and then show wherein their system (Islam) is deficient."[6] For years to come, these controversial issues triggered theological disputes and fears of syncretism.[7]

The Edinburgh conference was aware that, in different contexts, western Christian superiority was challenged by attempts to purify Islam. "This neo-Islam will appeal to patriotic feeling, and the removal of those features in the piety and morality of Islam that are now an offence may give it in this altered form a new lease of life."[8] Thus, the encounter between missionaries and Islamic communities generated an unexpected positive result. On one hand, it challenged Islam to purify itself and create a form of a neo-Islam and on the other it compelled Christian theologians to provide a new formulation of Christian dogmas of the Trinity, the incarnation and salvation thus making them understandable for a Muslim mind.[9] One of the recommendations of the sub-

---

[2] World Missionary Conference, 1910, *Report of The Commission IV, The Missionary Message in Relation to Non-Christian Religions* (Edinburgh & London: Oliphant, Anderson & Ferrier Publications), 1.

[3] Ibid., 4.

[4] Ibid., 132.

[5] Ibid., 140.

[6] Ibid., 141.

[7] Timothy Yates, *Christian Mission in the Twentieth Century* (Cambridge: Cambridge University Press, 1994), 94-124.

[8] World Missionary Conference, 1910, 132.

[9] Ibid., 136-7.

committee to missionaries was to learn in depth about Islam as a religion and to know the reality and culture of Muslim people among whom they were living.[10]

This advice was taken seriously, and many missionaries applied themselves to a rigorous study of the non-Christian faiths. This was especially evident at the conference of the International Missionary Council held in Tambaram, India, in 1938, during which the tension between syncretism and openness to other faiths was vehemently debated. In the first half of the 20th century, the ecumenical movement had not found institutional expression in the Middle East yet. Relations with Muslims were a subject of reflection within the various denominational families, but not in an institutionalized ecumenical setting. Protestants, in particular, attempted to discuss missionary work in predominantly Islamic societies in a broad coalition of mission agencies and local churches in a series of conferences.[11]

During the second half of the 20th century, the ecumenical approach to other faiths became less confrontational and gradually embraced the idea of open encounter. The impact of the Second World War, the threat of secularism, the rise of nationalism and the revival of Asian religions were important factors in reconfiguring the missionary scope.[12] The Word of God, the living faith of men, and nation building became interconnected fields in ecumenical thinking. "Stress was laid on the need to encourage and help Christians and Muslims to work together in nation building, and social welfare; such collaboration on the basis of mutual respect and common responsibility towards problems of radical social change would make possible deeper encounters which had hitherto been lacking."[13] The ecumenical Chang Mai Consultation on Dialogue with People of Living Faiths, in 1977, affirmed that dialogue is not a "betrayal of mission nor a 'secret weapon' but a way in which Jesus Christ can be confessed in the world today'."[14]

The following sections trace how this development from a reluctance to embrace dialogue to an enthusiasm and trust in dialogue as an integral part of mission developed within the context of Christian-Muslim dialogue, especially within the Middle East.

Ecumenical Landmarks and Dialogue with People of Other Faiths

Dialogue with the people of living faiths was one of the outcomes of the joining together of two main ecumenical streams, Life and Work and Faith and Order. These two came together on 23 August 1948 to create the World Council of

---

[10]Ibid.,138.

[11] Wilbert van Saane, "Middle East Study Centre Historical Report," in *A Hundred Years of Mission Cooperation: The Impact of the International Missionary Council 1921-2021*, ed. Risto Jukko (Geneva: WCC Publications, 2022), 259-262.

[12] S. Wesley Ariarajah, "Dialogue, Interfaith," in *Dictionary of the Ecumenical Movement,* ed. Nicolas Lossky et al. (Geneva: WCC Publications,2002), 312.

[13] Victor E. W. Hayward, "Guest Editorial," *International Review of Mission* 55:220 (1966), 403.

[14] Ariarajah, "Dialogue, Interfaith, " 315.

Churches. The WCC started as a predominantly Protestant initiative but soon the Eastern and Oriental Orthodox churches joined it as full members, while the Catholic Church remained an observer. With the integration of the International Missionary Council and the WCC at the New Delhi Assembly in 1961, the WCC became the main instrument of ecumenism and integrated different streams of mission into its programmatic scope, as well as their priorities and concerns.

The second landmark was the Second Vatican Council (1962-1965), where the dialogue with people of other faiths acquired a wider importance. The Declaration on the relation of the Catholic Church to the non-Christian religions, *Nostra Aetate* (proclaimed on 28 October 1965), stated: "The Church, therefore, exhorts her sons, that through dialogue and collaboration with the followers of other religions, carried out with prudence and love and in witness to the Christian faith and life, they recognize, preserve and promote the good things, spiritual and moral, as well as the socio-cultural values found among these men."[15] In the Declaration, the Council recognized Abraham as a common faith ancestor and highlighted the main points of overlap and divergence between Islam and Christianity.

The third major regional landmark was the establishment of the Middle East Council of Churches in 1974. The MECC continued, in the Middle East, the work that was started by the WCC before 1974 and soon emerged as a regional stakeholder of the Christian-Muslim dialogue legacy. The MECC emphasized the Arab context and Lebanon in particular as fields for Christian-Muslim encounters and possible cooperation with all the potentials and risks that this entailed.

With the ecumenical landscape drastically altered by the founding of the WCC and the MECC and by the new Catholic course set by the Second Vatican Council, the way was open to the churches to engage with people of other faiths in new ways, especially the way of official and representative dialogues.

Mapping the Major Initiatives

This section maps the pioneering encounters, foundational to the interfaith endeavour, that took place in the Middle East region. In this chronology, there is a need to address two distinct tracks:

Reflection among Christians on the Christian-Muslim Dialogues.

- The actual Christian-Muslim Dialogues sponsored by the WCC, facilitated and hosted by ecumenical regional bodies, mainly the MECC
- These events paved the way and fed into one another to create a platform for the launching of further interfaith endeavours in the Middle East and at the global level.

The first attempt to practically address the issue of mission in a multi-religious world setting took place in Broumana, Lebanon, in June 1966. This consultation

[15] Declaration on the Relation of the Church to Non-Christian Religions: Nostra Aetate, Proclaimed by His Holiness Pope Paul VI on 28 October 1965, accessed 14 November 2023, https://www.vatican.va/archive/hist_councils/ii_vatican_council/documents/vat-ii_decl_19651028_nostra-aetate_en.html.

among Christians from the Muslim world brought together 30 Christian scholars from 17 countries in Africa, the Middle East, South Asia and the West to "assess and consider this particular failure of the Church's life and mission today."[16] A new world was emerging after the Second World War. The UN Charter and the Universal Declaration of Human rights provided a legal framework for a new world order with strong secular and philosophical foundations. Moreover, the materialistic and secular ideologies at that time represented an alarming threat to world religions and Christianity in particular. The purpose of the meeting was to devise mutual cooperation and ways to promote productive meetings between Christians and Muslims. However, the participants expressed their disappointment that this issue was not on the agenda of the 4th WCC Assembly, which was held in Uppsala two years later, in 1968.[17]

From 2-6 March 1969, the WCC Faith and Order Commission invited 22 Muslims and Christians for four days of conversations in Cartigny, near Geneva.[18] The foundations for this meeting were laid during an earlier, smaller meeting in March 1968. The participants at the meeting spoke à titre personnel (speaking on his own behalf). The main theme was the necessity of dialogue in a changing world. The meeting pondered the commonalities and intercourse between religions and the challenges Christianity and Islam faced in the modern world. According to the participants, the aim of dialogue was to raise questions leading "each of the religions to a deepening and renewal of its spirituality," and "accepting and fulfilling common practical responsibilities."[19] The report of this meeting signalled the need for further study and consultation on the international level.

The first initiative that the WCC took to broaden the scope of interfaith encounters beyond Islam took place in the Middle East, in Ajaltoun, Lebanon, from 16–25 March 1970. This WCC consultation on "Dialogue between Men of Living Faiths", brought together 28 Christians, 3 Muslims, 3 Hindus and 4 Buddhists to converse and share personal views about recent experiences and future possibilities of dialogue. "The keynote of the consultation was the understanding that a full and loyal commitment to one's own faith did not stand in the way of dialogue. On the contrary, it was our faith which was the very basis of, and the driving force to, intensification of dialogue and a search for common action between members of different faiths in the various localities and situations in which they find themselves neighbours."[20]

The Ajaltoun meeting, though not formal or officially representative of these faith traditions, provided a major landmark in the evolution of the interreligious

---

[16] Victor E.W. Hayward, "Consultation among Christians from the Muslims World," in *Christians Meeting Muslims: WCC papers on 10 years of Christian Muslim dialogue*, comp. John B. Taylor (Geneva: WCC Publications, 1977), 12.

[17] Hayward, "Consultation among Christians from the Muslim World," 14.

[18] "Christian/Muslin Conversations, Summary of the Results Cartigny, March 2-6, 1969", in *Christians Meeting Muslims,* 67-70.

[19] Ibid., 68.

[20] "Dialogue between Men of Living Faiths: The Ajaltoun Memorandum," in *Christians Meeting Muslims,* 72.

dialogue in the 20th century. The participants came to the Ajaltoun meeting "not only to consult about inter-religious dialogue but to engage in it."[21] It also triggered the engagement of the WCC in further interfaith endeavours. The consultation on "Christians in Dialogue with Men of faiths" held in Zürich in May 1970 brought together 22 Roman Catholic, Orthodox, and Protestant theologians to consider and evaluate the Ajaltoun consultation and to see what lessons could be learned from such meetings for Christians in their continuing dialogues with people of other faiths. Their evaluation report of the Ajaltoun consultation was submitted to the WCC Central Committee, which met in Addis Ababa in 1971. As a result, the Central Committee decided to create a sub-unit on dialogue with people of other faiths. The concerted efforts of the WCC's sub-unit and the Vatican Secretariat for Non-Christians[22] provided a prominent platform for interfaith dialogue in the decades that followed. In this way, the institutionalization of the Christian-Muslim dialogue by ecumenical bodies served the development of real-life dialogical encounters and new insights in interfaith cooperation, to which we now turn.

In Search of Understanding and Cooperation: Christian and Muslim Contributions

This was the title of a consultation sponsored by the WCC and held in Broumana, Lebanon (12-18 July 1972).[23] 46 participants, half Christians half Muslims, from twenty countries, attended this consultation. Among them were prominent Christian theologians such as Georges Khodr, Wilfred Cantwell Smith, Stanley Samartha, Youakim Moubarac, and Lamin Sanneh. From the Muslim side, there were prominent figures of dialogue and proponents of openness and coexistence such as Imam Musa Sadr, who disappeared in Libya in 1978, and Sheikh Sobhi El Saleh, who was assassinated during the Lebanese civil war. The influence of such prominent participants from rich and diverse backgrounds is visible in the statement that came out of this meeting. The Broumana Memorandum, set a new course for Christian-Muslim dialogue. The report described what led the participants to meet, articulated their hopes in dialogue, and ended with suggestions for practical steps ahead at the national and local levels, to further the interreligious dialogue. According to this memorandum, the guiding principles for dialogue were: a frank witness, mutual respect, and religious freedom. Theological and spiritual renewal can pave the way for social renewal, the report stated. Christians and Muslims have the duty to remedy the wrongs of the society, even if they have to personally bear the consequences. Such interfaith attempts at ethical reform would not always be welcomed by others,

---

[21] Ariarajah, "Dialogue, Interfaith," 314.

[22] At this time, the Vatican engaged in a series of dialogue initiatives with the Supreme Council of Islamic Affairs in Cairo in Rome (16-20 December 1970), Tunisia (11-17 November 1974) and Libya (1-6 February 1976). The Secretariat for Non-Christians was renamed Pontifical Council for Interreligious Dialogue in 1998, and presently uses the name Dicastery for Interreligious Dialogue.

[23] "In Search of Understanding and Cooperation: Christian and Muslim Contributions, Broumana, Lebanon, July 1972," in *Christians Meeting Muslims*, 89-96.

the report acknowledged, but it was a risk that needed to be taken. Social justice, spirituality and dialogue should not be confined to particular social and political contexts and should be achieved by deliberate and self-conscious collaboration between Christians and Muslims. The Memorandum thus widened the settings of the dialogue beyond the formal meetings to include "social collaboration, intellectual cross-fertilization and vicarious participation in each other's devotional life."[24]

Christian Mission and Islamic *Da'wah*

The Ajaltoun meeting had identified mission and proselytism as special points of concern for interreligious dialogue. Responding to this, the WCC organized a consultation of Christians and Muslims concerning Christian mission and Islamic *da'wah* in Chambesy, Switzerland (26-30 June 1976). In his introductory note, Emilio Castro, who directed the Commission on World Mission and Evangelism and would later become the WCC's general secretary (1985-1992), affirmed that this consultation was based on the fact that both Islam and Christianity are missionary faiths and that in the fulfilment of their respective vocations they were faced with grievances from both sides.[25] The basic notion of freedom to practise one's religion had to be taken a step further, the participants realised. Both Islam and Christianity included an imperative to spread one's faith and exercise one's freedom "to convince and be convinced."[26] This freedom was acknowledged as an integral issue, essential to both religions.

To reflect the importance of this consultation, the October 1976 issue of the *International Review of Mission* (*IRM*) was co-edited and prefaced by a Muslim, Khurshid Ahmad[27] and a Christian, David Kerr.[28] Both voiced the dilemmas faced when Muslims and Christians try to reconcile the noble motives of the calling for the spread of their respective faiths with the grievances that were generated as a result, especially by Christian missionaries. About Christian missionaries, Ahmad wrote that "some of them might have been motivated by the best of spiritual intentions," but that "the overall Muslims experience of the Christian mission was such that it failed to commend itself as something noble and holy."[29] Kerr echoed this: "The absolute commitment of the Christian to mission and of the Muslim to *da'wah* has undoubtedly been one of the principal contributory factors to the tension, and at times conflict, which has so extensively

---

[24] "In Search of Understanding and Cooperation," in *Christians Meeting Muslims*, 93.

[25] "Consultation of Christians and Muslims Concerning Christian Mission and Islamic Da'wah," in *Christians Meeting Muslims,* 129.

[26] "Consultation of Christians and Muslims Concerning Christian Mission and Islamic Da'wah," 130.

[27] At the time, Khurshid Ahmad was Director General of the Islamic Foundation, Leicester, England.

[28] At the time, David A. Kerr served as Director of the Center for the Study of Islam and Christian-Muslim Relations, Selly Oak, Birmingham.

[29] Khurshid Ahmad, "Guest Editorial," *International Review of Mission* 65:260 (1976), 367.

characterized the relationships between Christianity and Islam."[30] *Da'wah* or 'invitation' in Arabic is the call extended to all to embrace Islam as the true religion of Allah (God). The *IRM* issue included some of the conference papers, in which the authors reflected on the Christian experience of Islamic *da'wah* and the Muslim experience of Christian mission.

The final statement of the Chambésy consultation addressed freedom of religion, moral wrongs committed in the name of spreading one's faith, the abuse of *diakonia*, and the importance of the family and community, which were often affected by mission and *da'wah*. The Muslim and Christian participants agreed on the following points:

- To uphold "the full liberty to convince and be convinced..., to maintain his/her religious integrity in obedience to his/her religious principles and in faithfulness to his/her religious identity."
- To uphold the freedom to practise religion, i.e to live according to religious laws in the family and to educate the children of the community according to religious principles in schools. This freedom was established as a right not linked to any majority or minority considerations but "as equal citizens."
- To acknowledge the colonial history, political agendas, proselytism and abuses of *diakonia* services, which had been sources of mistrust and suspicion hindering the way forward.
- To view *diakonia* as an expression of unselfish love, *agape*, and respecting the dignity and integrity of the people concerned, which was thought to cleanse the atmosphere of mistrust and "orient them towards mutual recognition and co-operation worthy of the two great religions."[31]

While there was an invitation to share in each other's festivities, sharing in worship was a sensitive topic. The participants made a distinction between formal worship (for Muslims prayer, *salat*) and supplication (*du'a'*). "Some of us have been willing to allow silent presence at each other's worship times. Some of us have shared in prayer in supplication and meditation and have prayed for each other since we all pray to the One God and believe that He is in our dialogue."[32]

Finally, this conference was instrumental in creating a solid base to carry this issue further and deeper. The follow-up was envisaged as a process that needed prayers from the Muslim and Christian communities, so that "the relations between their people may soon blossom into spiritual fellowship, to the glory of God alone."[33]

---

[30] David A. Kerr, "Guest Editorial," *International Review of Mission* 65:260 (1976), 370.

[31] "Statement of the Conference on 'Christian Mission and Islamic Da'wah,' Chamésy, June 1976," in *Christians Meeting Muslims*, 138-141.

[32] Ibid., 146.

[33] Ibid., 141.

Ecumenism: Proclamation in Dialogue

This survey of interfaith meetings shows that, gradually, dialogue was no longer viewed as contrary or detrimental to Christian mission and proclamation, but commensurate with it. Dialogue was even presented as a mode of proclamation. It took many encounters in which the dialogue partners grew in mutual appreciation and understanding of the other faith. Building on St Peter's words to Cornelius that "in every nation everyone who fears him and does what is right is acceptable to him,"[34] openness towards the religious other becomes a way to discern, as the reflection of Christian theologians in Zürich on the Ajaltoun 1970 consultation articulated, what "God is saying to us in Christ."[35] It was a faith journey in discernment of the signs of time.

The Zürich meeting also reflected on the role of the Holy Spirit in interreligious encounters. The Spirit's work was especially described in terms of love. The Ajaltoun text expressed faith that the Holy Spirit would be the enabler to engage in dialogue with full openness to the truth. Dialogue, in this context of ecumenism, was like proclamation. It became a way to communicate, to transform and be transformed. The aim of dialogue was seen as a means of expressing love which makes the truth creative. Love was not seen as immune to abuse and misinterpretation; it was acknowledged as a vulnerable attitude. But it was also acknowledged that true love has a transformative power. Love was needed for dialogue, for it "casts out fear"[36] and makes the truth life giving. The mission of the church was described as "the calling of the whole church to work for the unity of mankind."[37] Consequently, interfaith dialogue was no longer viewed as a betrayal of mission but rather as a new tool for mission "which neither betrays the commitment of the Christians nor exploits the confidence and the reality of men of other faiths."[38]

Where Are We Now?

As we have argued, The Broumana Memorandum (1972) set, to a large extent, the course for the subsequent Christian-Muslim engagement within the ecumenical movement. It highlighted the fact that the dialogue was not intended to suppress differences but rather to explore them openly and self-critically between committed and responsible individuals with genuine commitment to dialogue as a process of mutual enrichment and in full obedience to God. As this section demonstrates, this had practical, theological and institutional fruits.

First, practical guidelines for dialogues facilitated future Christian-Muslim encounters. The Cartingy Aide-Mémoire[39] was significant as it articulated a basic

---

[34] Acts 10:35.

[35] "Christians in Dialogue with Men of Other Faiths," in *Christians Meeting Muslims*, 22.

[36] 1 John 4:18.

[37] "Christians in Dialogue with Men of Other Faiths," 23.

[38] Ibid., 24.

[39] "Planning meeting for next steps in Christian Muslim Dialogue, aide-memoire of meeting held 19-22 October 1976, Cartigny," in *Christians Meeting Muslims*, 143-15.

code of conduct in the form of dos and don'ts. It provided a list of what each partner in dialogue should aim to achieve and to avoid. This document introduced the concept of "living in dialogue," which combined the ethos of faithfulness to God's calling and the praxis of dialogue as an incarnation of the proclamation here and now. Dialogue was viewed as all-inclusive, encompassing all human beings, males and females, young and old. It focused on three main areas: education, family life and worship and prayer.

Second, the interfaith dialogues helped theologians develop their understanding of Christian mission and their theologies of the religions. In the ecumenical movement, mission was now understood as a proclamation of the gospel in dialogue with people of other faiths. Some of the Middle Eastern participants in these meetings embarked on theological and academic attempts to contextualize the concept of mission within their local church traditions. We briefly consider the ideas of Georges Khodr and Youakim Moubarac, as they illustrate how their participation in interfaith dialogue influenced their theologies of the religions and especially their view of Christian-Muslim relations.

Bishop Khodr pondered the Orthodox understanding of mission. For him, witness was the key concept of mission. It was "the right of all people to hear the gospel."[40] Rooted in the biblical and Eucharistic reality of the church, mission was "to witness outside the sanctuary."[41] Proclamation "introduces the world to the communal life of the Trinity."[42] This ecumenical and comprehensive approach will only acquire its full dimension when it encounters the religious others, in the context of the Middle East mostly Muslims. Khodr believed that a church can speak to the heart of Islam when it empties, impoverishes and frees itself of its ethnic and intellectual superiority. To Khodr, the core issue was to search for "the traces of Christ in the Koran as well as in the tradition of Islam, especially within the Sufi heritage."[43]

Fr Youakim Moubarac took a similar path when he examined evangelization and dialogue in light of the Muslim-Christian experience. He outlined three main attitudes towards Islam: the scientific approach, practical participation, and the spiritual calling.[44] The first was a theoretical approach that dealt with the question of legitimacy of Islam as an Abrahamic religion of universal nature. The second focused on the long history of the joint struggle with reason and philosophy. The third dealt with the heart and Sufism, with a special emphasis on Arabism as a melting point between Muslims and Christians who were together facing the agony of Palestine.[45] Moubarac presented these ideas at the MECC general assembly held in February 1975 under the theme: "Evangelization and Dialogue."

---

[40] Georges Khodr, "The orthodox Understanding of Mission", in *Orthodox Youth and the Ecumenical Movement*, ed. Nicolae Mihaita (Geneva: WSCF Publications, 1978), 49.

[41] Ibid., 50.

[42] Ibid., 51.

[43] Ibid., 54.

[44] Youakim Moubarac, *Al-Kirāza Wal-Hiwār 'ala Daw' al-Ikhtibār al-Islāmiy al-Masihy* (Beirut: An-Nour Publications, 1977), 9.

[45] Ibid., 35-36.

Third, the dialogues that took place in the Middle East bore lasting institutional fruit. The MECC worked as a catalyst for interfaith initiatives that were later institutionalized. The MECC capitalized on the pioneering work of the World Student Christian Federation (WSCF) Middle East secretariat that had opened in the mid-sixties. Ecumenical figures like Gabriel Habib, who was the WSCF Middle East Secretary and in 1975 became MECC General Secretary, provided an ecumenical continuity from the WCC and the WSCF to the MECC. The MECC acquired its own Middle Eastern identity, representing a broader membership than the WCC, especially through the inclusion of the Eastern and Oriental Catholics. This identity was reflective of the rich church diversity in the Arab region and expressive of the solidarity with the Muslims around issues of peace and justice in general and Palestine in particular. There were three major specialized organizations that emerged from these Christian-Muslim encounters. The first was the Islamic-Christian National Dialogue Committee that was established as a result of the 1993 spiritual summit in the Maronite Patriarchate in Bkerke. The second was the Arab Working Team for Muslim-Christian Dialogue that was established in 1995. The third was the Lebanese Encounter for Dialogue. In addition, a memorandum of understanding was signed by the MECC and the International Islamic Forum for Dialogue in 2004 to foster creative forms of cooperation between these two faith-based organizations. These institutional forms of cooperation may be viewed as a fruit of the dialogue process that has been described in this paper.

The dialogue with people of other faiths as a tool for nation-building found its full fruition in the work of the MECC at the end of the Lebanese civil war of 1975-1989. Beginning in May 1990, and after the signing of the Taif Agreement, which was adopted as a basis for reconciliation and reform in Lebanon by members of the Lebanese parliament in 1989, the MECC brought together Lebanese intellectuals from different sects, regions, affiliations, and backgrounds.[46] The title of the first Lebanese Encounter meeting was "Common Living and the Future of Lebanon." The participants at the meeting discussed the issues of national unity, national sovereignty, Lebanon's relationship with the surrounding countries, and the political system that was most suitable for the Lebanese state and society.

Coexistence, national sovereignty and civil peace are intertwined. They affect each other and, therefore, need to be considered together in any approach to defuse a conflict or resolve a crisis. A strong tradition of Christian-Muslim dialogue, as it developed through the ecumenical movement and especially the WCC and the MECC, may provide a valve, whenever sectarian violence threatens to spiral out of control and hostilities exacerbate between the components of the national fabric. The ecumenical institutions were catalysts and helped bring together Christians and Muslims to reflect and offer insights on pressing issues at the national and global levels. In many cases, these ecumenical dialogues were a kind of safety net for the national and regional dialogues and, as such, they were vital for the stability of multi-confessional communities.

[46] The First Lebanese Encounter took place in Limassol, Cyprus on 5-8 May 1990.

Finally, it is important to emphasize the concept of "Living in Dialogue", which implies that dialogue goes beyond the institutional and becomes a state of mind and a pattern of behaviour. This latent need for engagement between people across religious divides will undoubtedly build up its own momentum and will become a driving force for the interfaith encounter that will grow day by day and will yield new joint ventures between Christians and Muslims at various levels.

The Christian-Muslim encounters that were described in this chapter have provided a platform for exchange of ideas, expression of fears, and aspirations. As a result of these dialogues, many participants such as Kenneth Cragg, Georges Khodr, Youakim Moubarac became distinguished specialists in interfaith studies and advocates of dialogue and cooperation across religious divides.

Mission and Education: A Call from the Land of the Cedars to the Middle East – A Catholic Perspective

Ziad Fahed

Introduction

> The righteous will flourish like a palm tree, they will grow like a cedar of Lebanon; planted in the house of the Lord, they will flourish in the courts of our God. They will still bear fruit in old age, they will stay fresh and green, proclaiming, "The Lord is upright; he is my Rock, and there is no wickedness in him." (Psalm 92:12-15).

With these words the psalmist describes the mission of the righteous and how to grow despite all sorts of challenges, similar to a cedar tree that continues growing in hot and cold seasons, spreading its roots deeper and its branches wider and wider while remaining rooted in the court of God. Similar to the cedar's mission, educational institutions are called to remain rooted and stay fresh and green despite challenges and difficulties.

In Lebanon, education is one of the main pillars of society. Decades of academic experience, rooted and solid curriculums, competent professors and administrators have given the Lebanese educational system a strong reputation both at the regional and international levels. This prestigious level was achieved mainly due to Christian missionaries, who founded and sustained numerous educational institutions and spread their mission through these institutions. As a result, the Christian educational institutions have become an indispensable part of the mission of the churches.

Recent challenges, such as the Covid 19 pandemic and the multilayered political and economic crises (2020-2023), have severely impacted the Lebanese educational system. To be more precise, education in Lebanon was negatively affected by the steep devaluation of the Lebanese currency,[1] the Beirut blast (August 4, 2020), which destroyed half of the capital including many schools and universities; as well as two years of lockdowns in which schools switched to online learning. Other factors exacerbated the situation: power cuts, unstable internet connections, lack of technological devices, parents at work and children alone at home, and family income reductions of, in some cases, 95 percent, due to the economic crisis. Efforts of teachers to reshape curricula and pedagogical approaches, adapting them to the new situation of the students in class, online, or in hybrid forms notwithstanding, the educational sector is in danger. Lebanon risks an exodus of qualified teachers and students with wealthy parents.

---

[1] Emilie Madi and Mohamed Azakir, "As economy worsens, Lebanese juggle dizzying rates for devalued pound," *Reuters*, 19 March 2023, accessed 3 April 2023, https://www.reuters.com/world/middle-east/economy-worsens-lebanese-juggle-dizzying-rates-devalued-pound-2023-03-19.

In addition to this external threat to education in Lebanon, one can also acknowledge the existence of internal threats, such as a loss of explicit visible Christian identity and the commercialization of schools that once began as missionary institutions. Because many Christian educational institutions opened their doors to welcome a wide diversity of students, especially in predominantly Muslim environments, they had to "adjust" their curriculum and reduce Christian activities. While this was an acceptable compromise for those who contended that Christian schools and universities had become a convenient way of raising money for their religious communities, it was less satisfactory for Christian schools who sought to preserve their Christian identity, and were forced to soft-pedal it in order not to offend the Muslim students, families, and environment. They felt that their institutions had lost their Christ-centeredness. Despite such dilemmas, the Lebanese Christian educational system "has been acknowledged for endorsing missions and values with the aim of building lifelong learners and patriotic citizens."[2]

In the face of these external and internal threats, the Christian communities of Lebanon seek not just to sustain the Christian educational system but also their unique Christian mission. This chapter begins by tracing the historical background of the Lebanese educational system, and then proceeds to identify building blocks for a more robust and Christ-centred perception of mission through Christian educational institutions. While focusing on the Lebanese context, our remarks and reflections are also applicable to Christian educational institutions in other parts of the Middle East. This chapter may be read as a call from the Land of the Cedars to Christian communities across the region.

This chapter argues that Catholic theology, and more precisely Catholic Social Teaching, provides a pathway for schools and universities to a more Christ-centred, inclusive, and embracing mission. It presents a multifaceted and dynamic response to the unique context and challenges faced by the local Christian community. Catholic Social Teaching could be a solid, interactive bridge between the churches in Lebanon and the Middle East, so that, together, they can answer their initial call. It is a call of faithful witness to the gospel of Christ in the midst of a diverse and often divided society, seeking richer social engagement and encouraging dialogue, collaboration and understanding while respecting the richness of each member of the local community.

The following specific questions are addressed in this chapter: How can the mission of Christian institutions be more Christ-centred and accessible to those who are in need? How does the Christian intellectual, academic tradition contribute to the nation's intellectual culture? In relation to that, how do Christian social and moral teaching contribute to the nation's development? How can those involved in Christian educational work, while respecting the ethos of each institution, develop and strengthen an ecumenical missionary spirit within each educational institution? And, finally, how can the churches play a

---

[2] Maha Mouchantaf, "Lebanese Catholic schools: past achievements and contemporary challenges in times of economic distress and COVID 19 pandemic," *International Studies in Catholic Education*, 7 January 2021. DOI: 10.1080/19422539.2020.1858636.

constructive role within the schools and universities, helping them to remain faithful to their missionary call?

Historical Background

Lebanon's ethnic and religious diversity inevitably played a role in shaping its educational system. A country of 10,452 square kilometres, Lebanon has 18 different religious confessions officially recognized by the Lebanese constitution. Historically, some of these religious groups found refuge in Lebanon's mountainous terrain away from persecution, where they could freely practise and share their political and religious beliefs. They preferred a harsh life in the mountains to the comfort of the city, in order to preserve and defend their religious beliefs, their cultures, and their cherished freedom. During the French mandate, religious freedom became a distinguishing characteristic of the country and Lebanon became a "mosaic of religions" that encompasses a plurality of cultures and religions.[3] Two major religious groups are prominent: the Christians, including Orthodox, Catholics, Maronites, Protestants, and Armenian Orthodox, and the Muslims, including the Sunnis, Shiites, Alawites, and Druze.

Christian schools were pioneers and many were established by European religious orders and congregations during the 18th and 19th centuries, as well as by American missionaries who came to the region for evangelization purposes. The Pontifical Maronite College in Rome for Maronite priestly formation, founded by Pope Gregory XIII in 1584, sent many gifted and passionate priests back to Lebanon to open schools across their homeland. Idir Ouahes remarks that, as a result of the Ottoman Empire's policy, the situation by the start of the French Mandate was marked by a clear split in educational policies attaching religious denominations to regional powers.[4] Catholic establishments, whether sponsored by French or Italian power, followed a more traditional emphasis on rote learning. Protestant education was a bit more open, with institutions such as the American University in Beirut having an impact on a whole generation of Arab intellectuals. Protestant and Catholic networks increasingly competed with each other and, during the Mandate period, made significant inroads into the Syrian interior.[5] Minority groups also organized their own religious education, the outstanding example being that of the Jewish Alliance Israelite Universelle, which opened a school in Beirut in the 1870s.[6] Ouahes observes that Russia had

---

[3] Ziad Fahed, "Lebanon," in *Encyclopedia of Global Religion*, ed. Mark Juergensmeyer and Wade Clark Roof (London: SAGE Publications, 2012). http://sk.sagepub.com/reference/globalreligion/n406.xmly.

[4] Idir Ouahes, *Syria and Lebanon under the French Mandate: Cultural Imperialism and the Workings of Empire* (London and New York: I.B. Tauris, 2018), 117-137.

[5] Henry Diab and Lars Wåhlin, "The Geography of Education in Syria in 1882. With a Translation of 'Education in Syria' by Shahin Makarius, 1883," Geografiska *Annaler* 65:2 (1983), 105-128. https://doi.org/10.2307/490939.

[6] Michael M. Laskier, "Aspects of the activities of the Alliance Israelite Universelle in the Jewish communities of the Middle East and North Africa: 1860-1918," *Modern Judaism* 3:2 (May 1983), 147-171.

a long relationship with Orthodox communities in the Syrian interior. Despite this diverse range of activities, French missionary involvement had the longest and most widespread influence, particularly in the Lebanese littoral.

Initial Catholic involvement began as a result of 17th century interactions between the Maronites and the French king. In 1835, the Lazarist Order founded the College of Saint Joseph, the oldest French school in the region. The Lazarists had an intimate connection with the Orient, having been founded by St Vincent de Paul, who had been a slave in North Africa and Ottoman Istanbul. Following the example of the Lazarists, myriad Catholic orders, such as the Jesuits, the White Fathers, the Marists, and the Sisters of Charity became involved. Higher education was also the result of missionary activity. Following the American University of Beirut, which was founded by American Protestant missionaries in 1866, the Jesuits founded Saint Joseph University in 1875.

Today, schools in Lebanon range from public and UNRWA (United Nations Relief and Works Agency for Palestine Refugees) to fully paid and semi-paid private schools. The latest statistics show the following numbers: 1236 public schools (36.5 percent of the total number of students), 65 UNRWA schools (3.5 percent), 331 free private schools (11 percent), and 1164 private schools (48.8 percent). Of Lebanon's one million students, 70 percent attend private schools, and according to the General Secretariat of Catholic schools, about 20 percent of private school students attend Catholic Schools.[7] Currently, there are 362 Catholic schools affiliated with the General Secretariat.

Most Christian schools have adopted a trilingual educational system, which increases the possibilities of excelling in official exams such as the French Baccalaureate and enhances the chances of acceptance into foreign universities. Their curricula are distinguishable by their openness to science, modern technology, and exposure to the western world. Maintaining high standards in these areas has strengthened the educational mission of these schools. It has also encouraged their leaders to provide the Lebanese community with a futuristic vision that helps in bonding the religious, cultural, and intellectual dimensions of Lebanon.

In addition, it is worth emphasizing that many Catholic, Orthodox and Protestant schools are no longer or not at all situated in Christian majority cities, towns, villages, and neighbourhoods, but are located in regions that have predominantly Muslim populations. Examples are the Antonine School of Nabatieh in the south of the country, where more than 90 percent of the students are Muslim. In the Orthodox School of Saint Elijah in Tripoli more than 75 percent of the students are Muslims. 99 percent of the students enrolled in the Maronite Bishop's school in Jabal Mohsen are Muslims. These examples demonstrate that the churches are convinced that their schools can have a meaningful presence in these predominantly non-Christian regions. Despite its strong establishment, mission, and omnipresence in diverse areas across

---

[7] Doreen Abi Raad, "Future of Lebanon's Catholic Schools at Risk under New Salary Rules," *Catholic News Service*, 12 October 2018, accessed 3 April 2023, https://cnewa.org/future-of-lebanons-catholic-schools-at-risk-under-new-salary-rules/.

Lebanon, the Christian school, with its rich historical background, is facing several challenges, to which we now turn.

The Mission of Christian Educational Institutions

A Christ-Centred Mission

For several decades, Lebanese Christian schools and universities have consistently demonstrated a commitment to educational excellence. They have aimed at spreading, with Christian and human principles and values, hope among young people and preparing them for a better future. Moreover, they have welcomed students of different religious denominations and have worked to form good citizens for tomorrow, loyal and faithful to the country. We now consider the question how these schools express their distinctive Christian heritage and mission. How do they seek to remain Christ-centred in their mission?

A theological understanding on the strategic role of education is reflected in many Catholic teachings. According to the Pope Paul VI's Declaration *Gravissimum Educationis* (1965), education is an inalienable right and serves the ultimate goal of humankind, because "a true education aims at the formation of the human person in the pursuit of his ultimate end and of the good of the societies of which, as man, he is a member, and whose obligations, as an adult, he will share."[8] Describing Christian education more specifically, he added "a Christian education does not merely strive for the maturing of a human person…, but has as its principal purpose this goal: that the baptized, while they are gradually introduced to the knowledge of the mystery of salvation, become ever more aware of the gift of Faith they have received, and that they learn in addition how to worship God the Father in spirit and truth (cf. John 4:23)."[9]

Being called to be Christ-centred institutions means much more than simply providing a religion class among many other courses. Instead, by integrating the Christian ethos within the institution, inside and outside the classroom, the schools acknowledge Christ as the Redeemer, Restorer, and the Lord. All of humankind is made in his image. Within an educational institution, this is reflected in how the educational institution deals with students, parents, and staff. It is also expressed by leaving no one behind, reflecting the gospel values and principles, answering the call for creating a visible human fraternity, and healing the wounds of the world. In other words, all liberal arts courses, whether history, art, music, literature, mathematics, or science, should be taught in the light of God's existence and his revelation to humanity through his Son, Jesus Christ. Because we are created in God's image (Gen. 1:26-27), Christian educational institutions must appreciate the goodness he has made in the world.

Being a Christ-centred institution also requires extending an invitation to students to think critically and never spare any effort to seek the truth, so that

---

[8] Declaration on Christian Education 'Gravissimum Educationis' Proclaimed by His Holiness Pope Paul VI on October 28, 1965, 1.

[9] Ibid., 2.

they "may know Him, and the power of His resurrection, and the fellowship of His sufferings" (Phil. 3:10) and "teaching them to observe all things" and to know that Jesus is with them always, "even unto the end of the world" (Matt. 28:20). Among the biggest tragedies of our societies is the culture of blind followers, which makes it more urgent to prepare the students to understand how to adopt a critical approach, which transforms them into peace builders and helps them to be the change they want to see.

Christian educational institutions are called to make the gospel visible and accessible through their policies and their cultures of life, loving each one. This will open the gates for students to live in continual harmony with God, a lifelong process through which God transforms them to become like Jesus. They work on the assumption that Christlikeness is the purpose of human life. As the Apostle Paul writes, "For those whom he foreknew, he also predestined to be conformed to the image of his Son, in order that he might be the firstborn within a large family" (Rom. 8:29). They seek to form communities that are like families in order to form their members in such a way that they are able to say, with the Apostle Paul: "I am crucified with Christ; and it is no longer I who live, but it is Christ who lives in me. And the life I now live in the flesh I live by the faith of the Son of God, who loved me and gave himself for me" (Gal. 2:19-20).

Even if many Lebanese Christian educational institutions are putting some of these elements into practice, we believe that more needs to be done in this direction. The internal and external challenges mentioned above while negatively affecting the Christian ethos, may also be viewed as an opportunity to rethink the mission and culture of Christian institutions and open avenues toward promoting Christian values within the educational institutions. I will now describe in more detail what such a Christ-centred educational approach looks like according to Catholic Social Teaching, focusing on Integral Human Development, human dignity, and solidarity.

A Mission Focused on Integral Human Development

In Catholic Social Teaching, Christian educational institutions are important instruments in spreading Integral Human Development that promotes the good of every person in a wholistic manner. Catholic thinkers and leaders have called upon educational institutions to take it as a guiding principle. Integral Human Development points to a goal and a process of moving together in solidarity. It comprises cultural, academic, economic, political, social, and spiritual dimensions. Lebanese schools and universities have the task of translating this call into a process that takes on the difficulties and challenges of today's society. In 1967, Pope Paul VI introduced in his encyclical letter *Populorum Progressio* the concept of integral development, writing that "development cannot be limited to mere economic growth. In order to be authentic, it must be complete: integral, that is, it has to promote the good of every man and of the whole man."[10] In the 1987 encyclical *Sollicitudo Rei Socialis*, Pope John Paul II, stated: "In this pursuit of Integral Human Development, we can also do much with the members

---

[10] 'Populorum Progressio': Encyclical of Pope Paul VI on the Development of Peoples, 29 March 1967, 14.

of other religions. Collaboration in the development of the whole person and every human being is, in fact, a duty of all towards all, and must be shared by the four parts of the world: East and West, North and South."[11] Accordingly, Lebanese Christian educational institutions have a mission to promote Integral Human Development by inviting pupils and members of the institutions to real participation in the fullness of life, which includes enjoyment of family, society, and nature, as well as the gifts that come from learning new things, from earning a dignified living, and contributing to a rich civic life and building peaceful societies.

As a cross-disciplinary approach, Integral Human Development allows Christian educational institutions to create dynamic engagement based on human dignity and cooperation to help heal the wounds of Lebanon's violent past and its difficult present. As the quotation from Pope John Paul II demonstrates, it also allows for building interactive bridges among religious groups, and it values cultural diversity within the country. For that reason, Integral Human Development provides a good foundation to address contemporary challenges and achieve sustainable development.

Educational institutions that incorporate the principles of Integral Human Development will shape their curriculums in such a way as to focus on personal well-being in a context of just and peaceful relationships. Such a curriculum seeks to foster the cultural, economic, political, social, and spiritual wholeness of the students – a wholeness that will equip students to be more committed toward the common good. In Lebanese Catholic schools and universities, a move towards the Integral Human Development approach is already discernible. Most Catholic educational institutions include pastoral work and offer a rich programme of community service activities and other extracurricular activities.

While there are encouraging signs, the implementation of Integral Human Development is facing tremendous obstacles. The deep economic crisis since 2019 has forced the schools to shift their priorities to their immediate needs, especially the increase of financial aid to students. As a result, budgets for cultural activities, including conferences, talks, travel, and publications have either decreased or been completely cancelled in many institutions. On-campus political debates on the current challenges are often not authorized by the universities, due to the tensions that such debates may create. We may conclude that efforts to incorporate Integral Human Development in the schools and universities are still at an initial stage and are quite vulnerable given the present state of the Lebanese economy and society.

A Mission Based on Catholic Social Teaching

A number of principles from Catholic Social Teaching are especially relevant to the current social, political, and economic situation of Lebanon and the Middle East. Revisiting these principles may help strengthen the Christian identity amidst the challenging time that the region is facing. It may especially help

---

[11] John Paul II, 'Sollicitudo Rei Socialis': To the Bishops, Priests, Religious Families, Sons and Daughters of the Church and All the People of Good Will, for the Twentieth Anniversary of 'Populorum Progressio,' 32.

teachers, staff, administrators, and students in leadership positions to be guided by a Christian ethos, as they seek to fulfil their mission through development, scholarships, academic excellence, integrity, and pastoral care.

The fundamental principles that are of particular importance are: human dignity, subsidiarity, and solidarity. These three cornerstones contribute to the common good, and are much needed in the Lebanese context and its educational system, because of the sectarian make-up in Lebanese society and the collapse of social contract. Schools and universities are an appropriate 'training ground' for these principles, and students who have practised them there will be inclined to implement them on the work floor and in political life. The strategic value of these three cornerstones matches with the objectives of Catholic educational institutions whose mission is to prepare students for leadership in tomorrow's society. A successful preparation of the students must start from and within the educational journey, in order to shape leaders who are prepared to shoulder the full responsibility of the society of tomorrow.

The first principle, human dignity, has been discussed in the previous section. The principle of subsidiarity puts a proper limit on government by insisting that no higher level of organization should perform any function that can be handled efficiently and effectively at a lower level of organization, by human persons, who, individually or in groups, are closer to the problems on the ground. The principle of subsidiarity lies at the heart of a stable social order by fostering a personal responsibility that naturally accompanies individual liberty. It ensures that personal interest is not placed in opposition to societal interest by bringing individual desires and the demands of the common good into fruitful harmony. The common good is understood as that which meets and fulfils the interests of all people by making decisions and taking actions that benefit everyone. As Pope Benedict XVI said, it is "the totality of social conditions allowing persons to achieve their communal and individual fulfilment."[12] According to Vivencio Ballano, the common good "is concerned with the social welfare of all citizens, rich or poor."[13] The Lebanese interfaith experience is a case in point: it involves building interreligious bridges and promoting social harmony and building a society that values religious diversity, while the most vulnerable are the focus point of this cooperation. The common good is realised through the church's active involvement in providing social services irrespective of their denominations or background. Thus, it is mainly achieved through the application of policies and laws that preserve people's freedoms and dignity. In this way, the principles of subsidiarity and human dignity are interrelated: a proper implementation of subsidiarity safeguards human dignity, because it respects the individual's contribution to society on all levels.

---

[12] Pope Benedict XVI, Address to the Participants in the 14th Session of the Pontifical Academy of Social Sciences, 3 May 2008, accessed 3 April 2023, https://w2.vatican.va/content/benedict-xvi/en/speeches/2008/may/documents/hf_ben-xvi_spe_20080503_social-sciences.html.

[13] Vivencio Ballano, "Catholic Social Teaching, Theology, and Sociology: Exploring the Common Ground," *Religions* 10:10 (2019), 557. https://doi.org/10.3390/rel10100557.

We now turn to a rather elaborate discussion of the third principle, solidarity, in the context of Lebanon and the Middle East. A key imperative for Christian educational institutions is to promote the call for solidarity between people and different cultures, and to promote the rights and development of all peoples "across communities, nations, and the world, irrespective of national boundaries."[14] The more schools and universities orient their students toward discovering the value of being interconnected and the social nature of human beings, the deeper they can go within their own mission "for by his innermost nature man is a social being, and unless he relates himself to others, he can neither live nor develop his potential."[15]

Schools and universities can also promote solidarity by embracing cultural diversity within their institutions. The concept of "diversity" is mentioned clearly in the mission statements of the majority of the Christian schools and universities in Lebanon. This showed a real understanding, commitment of the educational system in terms of understanding how diversity and solidarity are interlinked. Having a diverse community of students, staff, and faculty is at the same time a source of pride for many Lebanese Christian institutions.

The interconnectedness of students in schools and universities promotes solidarity, as in the words of Pope Benedict XVI, it is "the virtue enabling the human family to share fully the treasure of material and spiritual goods."[16] The American Catholic scholar William Byron places the "love-your-neighbour" commandment in the framework of an interdependent universe.[17] In other words, solidarity is feeling with others, living with them, taking care of them, and helping them. It is what binds people together even amid differences. Solidarity is essential in every society because it joins people together and, in the words of Ignatian spiritual director Karen Wright, it is "the fabric for all authentic relationships."[18]

Within the complicated and fragmented Lebanese situation and a vibrant and diverse society, it is critical to elaborate on the concept of solidarity and how this can be translated, starting from the classroom. Anthropologist Diane Nelson took the idea of solidarity to another level by introducing critical solidarity or

---

[14] Jamie Davies, Duncan MacLaren, Laurie Needham, and Anthony Steel, "Principles of Engagement on International Development Through the Lens of Catholic Social Teaching," Caritas Australia, 14 September 2010, accessed 3 April 2023, https://www.caritas.org.au/media/lqzfe32y/our-values-catholic-social-teaching.pdf.

[15] Pastoral Constitution on the Church in the Modern World 'Gaudium et Spes' Promulgated by His Holiness Pope Paul VI on 7 December 1965, 12.

[16] Benedict XVI, Address to the Pontifical Academy of Social Sciences, https://www.vatican.va/content/benedict-xvi/en/speeches/2008/may/documents/hf_ben-xvi_spe_20080503_social-sciences.html, accessed in January 2024.

[17] William J. Byron, "Ten building blocks of Catholic Social Teaching," *America: The Jesuit Review*, 31 October 1998, accessed 3 April 2023, https://www.americamagazine.org/faith/1998/10/31/10-building-blocks-catholic-social-teaching.

[18] Karen S. Wright, "The principles of Catholic Social Teaching: A guide for decision making from daily clinical encounters to national policy making," *The Linacre Quarterly* 84:1 (2017), 10–22. https://doi.org/10.1080/00243639.2016.1274629.

"fluidarity," which she defines as being "an attitude and practice that embraces the complexity of engaging the other in pluralized and ever-changing struggles."[19] Fluidarity is about urging individuals to accept differences and diversities to help others while constantly questioning one's own motives and drives. According to Matthew Maruggi, "fluidarity is solidarity challenged by difference."[20] The perception of "fluidarity" is relevant to the complexity of the Middle East educational system, in which interfaith and intercultural experience is an everyday reality. As Nelson argues, this is not just a cognitive but also a physical reality and fluidarity pushes a student to accept differences and diversities. In this way solidarity is translated into action.

Solidarity is also expressed in the struggle of the Christian schools and universities to include those who have limited financial resources. Given the current economic malaise, this is indeed a difficult issue for Christian schools, not just in Lebanon.[21] Making the schools accessible to all is a serious challenge but it protects the institutions from becoming elitist, accessible only to those who can afford high tuition fees. Christ-centredness also means providing education for the most vulnerable: students who cannot afford tuition, students with special needs, students who are undocumented, etc. As the financial situation is complicated within the schools and universities, international financial support may be solicited so that that no one is left behind.

Ultimately, solidarity is a spiritual virtue. "Carry each other's burdens, and in this way you will fulfil the law of Christ" (Gal. 6:2). The gospel highlights the need for solidarity, the encouragement to support one another and act in unity, reflecting the love and compassion of Christ in being there for each other and in action. In the pluralistic societies of the Middle East, schools and universities are the right platforms to open the gate toward discovering and teaching spiritual solidarity. In a context where cultural and religious minorities are at risk and under pressure, spiritual solidarity may lead to increased cooperation among the different cultural groups, so that they can together overcome the cultural and spiritual challenges. In this way spiritual solidarity can provide a platform for shared experiences, real dialogue of life, and foster freedom of religion and beliefs, toward a more inclusive society. Spiritual solidarity is recognizing "the richness and authenticity of the other's spiritual experience."[22] It aims to reconcile the students' worlds and priorities with their beliefs. It seeks to meet the students where they are today within their own social environment and to

---

[19] Diane Nelson, *A Finger in the Wound: Body Politics in Quincentennial Guatemala* (Berkeley, CA: University of California Press, 1999), 73.

[20] Matthew Maruggi, "Through solidarity to 'Fluidarity': Understanding Difference and Developing Change Agency through Narrative Reflection," *Teaching Theology & Religion*, 15:4 (2012), 307-322. https://doi.org/10.1111/j.1467-9647.2012.00824.x.

[21] This is also the case for Christian schools in Syria and Jordan.

[22] Claire Schaeffer-Duffy, "Lebanese Interfaith Group Grounds Work in 'Spiritual Solidarity' with the Other," *National Catholic Reporter*, 25 April 2016, accessed 9 January 2024, https://www.ncronline.org/preview/lebanese-interfaith-group-grounds-work-spiritual-solidarity-other.

assist them in bridging the gap.[23] In Lebanese society, the involvement of schools and universities in teaching spiritual solidarity is still much-needed. This process, which recognizes the richness and authenticity of each person's spiritual and theological experience, includes giving a place to "the other" in my theology and provides "a praxis by which we might respond to the most pressing and immediate humanitarian crises of our day."[24] It invites the students to develop their own spiritual and theological experiences, not as individuals living on their own island, but, on the contrary, it invites them to discover their interconnectedness and commonalities, as I have argued elsewhere.[25] Spiritual solidarity demonstrates that by combining their own experiences and critical thinking approaches, students can positively impact their local societies while discovering the richness of their cultural traditions and the cultural traditions of others. It opens the eyes of the participants and makes them realise that solidarity is doable through concrete actions that start from a classroom and reach out to others. What more can an educational system ask for?

Conclusion

If true education consists not in imposing from above but in accompanying people in their development, it is important to note that such a sharing started with God who "loved us first" (1 Jn. 4:19) and took the initiative to intervene by sending his only Son. This divine initiative, which leads to care, is also attested by the Prophet Ezekiel in Ezekiel 34: 11-12: "For thus says the Lord God: Behold, I, even I, will both search my sheep, and seek them out. As a shepherd seeks out his flock in the day that he is among his sheep that are scattered; so, will I seek out my sheep, and will deliver them out of all places where they have been scattered in the cloudy and dark day. Inspired by the divine initiative of love, the churches of the Middle East have established educational institutions that share in God's "loving" and "seeking out."

In the field of education, the Middle Eastern Church has a tradition that should be safeguarded. It is called to be an educator of individuals and people. Christian schools are called to participate effectively in the mission of the Church and to provide quality education. The various institutions must be faithful to their mission as Christian establishments by placing themselves above all at the disposal of the Christian community, and more broadly of the whole country, in a spirit of dialogue with every segment of society. This chapter has argued that Catholic Social Teaching offers guiding principles that help schools to serve the wider community while retaining their unique Christian identity. In the Middle Eastern context of religious, ethnic, and cultural diversity, the Christian educational system is called to reconcile faith and reason "to unite existentially

---

[23] Ziad Fahed, "Teaching Spiritual Solidarity through 'Human Books'," *Teaching Theology & Religion* 23:3 (2020), 202-208. DOI: 10.1111/teth.12551.

[24] Mark W. Potter, Solidarity as a Spiritual Exercise: A Contribution to the Development of Solidarity in the Catholic Social Tradition (PhD diss., Boston College, 2009), 169–176 and 180.

[25] Ziad Fahed, "Teaching Spiritual Solidarity through 'Human Books'."

by intellectual effort two orders of reality that too frequently tend to be placed in opposition as though they were antithetical: the search for truth, and the certainty of already knowing the fount of truth."[26]

Through its schools and universities, the church in the Middle East puts itself at the service of believers and of those who do not believe but are in a sincere search for the truth. The fact that Christian educational institutions profess their faith in the Author of truth does not prevent the church from respecting those who do not believe or those who adopt another religious tradition and from seeking together, through reason, the path that leads to the whole truth. At this point of our study, we can confirm that it is not the educational system that has a mission, but it is the "mission" that has educational institutions.

[26] 'Ex Corde Ecclesiae': Apostolic Constitution of the Supreme Pontiff John Paul II on Catholic Universities, 15 August 1990, 1, accessed January 2024, https://www.vatican.va/content/john-paul-ii/en/apost_constitutions/documents/hf_jp-ii_apc_15081990_ex-corde-ecclesiae.html.

Monasticism and Mission in the Middle East

Antoine Al Ahmar and Garen Yosolkanian

Introduction

Monasticism and mission may seem mutually exclusive terms. In the perception of many, monastic life is associated with withdrawal rather than outreach, contemplation rather than action. Monks and nuns are often viewed as people who avoid contact with the outside world and pray for it rather than actively seek to change it. However, a survey of the history of mission demonstrates the very opposite: in every century of its existence, monks and nuns have led the Christian church in mission and have contributed to the renewal of the lives of individuals, churches, and societies.[1]

This chapter considers the missionary contributions of monastic communities in the Middle East, whose landscape is dotted with monasteries. It is no exaggeration to say that nowhere else in world Christianity does monasticism play such a central role as in the Middle East. The Middle East is the cradle of Christian monasticism and has witnessed a paradoxical renewal of monastic life in the 20th century. While Christian communities went through periods of political and economic pressure and even decline, monastic life was reinvigorated and came into bloom yet again in various parts of the region.

From the myriad of monastic orders, we have selected three case studies that, in our view, bring out some key aspects of monastic mission in the 20th century. These are Armenian, Maronite, and Greek Catholic monasticism which reveal the central role of monks and nuns in the evangelization and education of faith communities, their exemplary love and care for the land, their preservation and innovation of the cultures of their communities, and above all their witness to evangelical values. This chapter also highlights areas of tension between monastic life and missionary engagement as they manifest themselves in Middle Eastern monasticism. Before presenting the case studies from the 20th century, a brief historical sketch of Middle Eastern monasticism is given.

Brief Historical Sketch

Monasticism in the region goes back to the earliest centuries of Christianity. Even before St Anthony and St Pachomius took to the desert of Egypt, one can speak of a proto-monachism or first asceticism.[2] Men and women withdrew to

---

[1] Stephen Bevans and Roger Schroeder, *Constants in Context: A Theology of Mission for Today* (Maryknoll, NY: Orbis Books, 2004), 366-368.

[2] Anna Poujeau, "Monastic Movements and Spirituality," in *Christianity in North Africa and West Asia*, ed. Kenneth R. Ross, Mariz Tadros and Todd M. Johnson (Edinburgh: Edinburgh University Press), 400.

the desert and lived ascetic lives.[3] From the 4th century onwards, monasticism became a more widespread phenomenon and gained in influence. Historians often present the ascendancy of monasticism as a reaction to the more settled and even privileged position of the church after Constantine's conversion. Many followed Anthony's example and lived in solitude. Others lived a cenobitic (community) life, of which Pachomius is considered the father; he and his followers organized separate communities for men and women.[4] The Egyptian and the Syrian traditions were initially quite distinct and developed independently. In Syria, ascetic practices included life in the open and stylitism.[5] Stylites lived, prayed and preached on elevated platforms on pillars in the countryside. The most notable among them was Simeon, whose pillar was located in the north of Syria. Asceticism was at once a path toward holiness and unity with God and a "criticism of ordinary society."[6] However, monastic and semi-monastic communities, such as the one organized by Macrina in Cappadocia in the 4th century, also reached out to underprivileged and vulnerable groups such as abandoned children. Scholars agree that the monastic movement profoundly influenced the churches from the 4th century into the Middle Ages both by their attraction as places of visitation and pilgrimage and by their outreach. Scholars also point to the missionary engagement of monks from the Middle East in that period, which reached all the way to China.[7]

In the Middle Ages, monasticism experienced decline in number and activity, but it was by no means eradicated.[8] As the Middle East, North Africa and Central Asia came under Islamic rule, the time of expansion ended. Christians were assigned an inferior *dhimmi*-status and, as part of that, monasteries had to pay taxes to the authorities. In times of persecution, they became a target of desecration, massacre, and destruction. Assyrian Christianity, in particular, experienced what one scholar calls a "dark night," in which the Mongols eradicated its monasteries from Central Asia and decimated them in Mesopotamia.[9] Nevertheless, many monasteries of various traditions continued to attract monks and nuns, particularly in areas with dense Christian populations like Syria and Lebanon. Sometimes they lived in so-called "double monasteries,"

---

[3] Herman Teule, "Syrische spiritualiteit en kloosterleven," in *Handboek Oosters Christendom*, ed. Herman Teule and Alfons Brüning (Leuven: Peeters, 2018), 750.

[4] Derwas J. Chitty, *The Desert a City: An Introduction to the Study of Egyptian and Palestinian Monasticism under the Christian Empire* (Crestwood, NY: St Vladimir's Press, 1995), 20-31.

[5] Shafiq AbouZayd, "Ascetic Movement in the East: Origins, Development and Dissemination; II. In Syria, Iraq and Palestine," in *Christianity: A History in the Middle East*, ed. Habib Badr, Suad Abou el Rouss Slim, and Joseph Abou Nohra (Beirut: Middle East Council of Churches, 2005), 385-407.

[6] Diarmaid McCulloch, *A History of Christianity* (London: Penguin, 2009), 200.

[7] See e.g. Arthur Vööbus, *History of Asceticism in the Syrian Orient, I: The Origins of Asceticism and Early Monasticism in the Near East* (Louvain: Secrétariat du CorpusSCO, 1958), 310-315.

[8] Otto F.A. Meinardus, *Two Thousand Years of Coptic Christianity* (Cairo and New York: The American University in Cairo Press, 1999), 64-66.

[9] Herman Teule, "De (Assyrische) Kerk van het Oosten," in *Handboek Oosters Christendom*, 180-181.

where monks and nuns occupied adjacent buildings, supported each other, and preserved liturgies, languages, knowledge, manuscripts and traditions. In the late Middle Ages and the early modern period, under Ottoman rule, monastic life had periods of bloom and decline, often depending on the nature of the centralized and regional governments. In some areas, ruined monasteries were renovated and new ones were built.[10] Networks of monasteries remained a vital source of strength and shared funding.[11] While no longer the chief centres of cultural activity, Orthodox monasteries continued to have important cultural, social and economic roles through which they strengthened the Christian communities and helped them survive in adversities.[12]

While western Catholic missionaries had sporadically been active in the Middle East since the Crusades, the establishment of the Sacred Congregation for the Propagation of the Faith (1622) heralded a more systematic and widespread Catholic missionary effort in the region. The work of Franciscans, Capuchins, Dominicans, Jesuits, and Carmelites among Christian communities entailed religious teaching, general education, translation of religious literature, retreats, and hospitality to travellers.[13] In the 19th century, European Catholic missionary efforts intensified and many orders founded monasteries, convents, schools, and medical facilities, making western Catholic presence more visible and durable. From the second half of the 19th century onward, female orders such as the Sisters of Charity and the Sisters of the Holy Family joined the missionary work in the Middle East and attracted substantial numbers of local women. Under the influence of the western missionary impulse, in the 17th and 18th centuries, a reformation of Eastern monastic life took place, leading to the formalization of Eastern Catholic orders, among whom the Order of the Lebanese Monks and the (also Maronite) Antonines were the most prominent. More will be said about this later. The founding of such orders associated with the Eastern Catholic churches continued in the 19th and 20th centuries. In the 19th century, Ottoman land reforms had favourable consequences for some monastic communities as their land holdings increased and were now viewed as inalienable.

Despite the relative stability during most of the Ottoman period, the number of Eastern and Oriental monks and nuns remained relatively modest and monasteries were vulnerable, except in Mount Lebanon. This vulnerability became especially evident during World War I. Fearing a growing nationalism among Christian communities, the Ottoman government organized massive deportations and unleashed massacres of Christian minorities, especially Armenians, Greeks, Assyrians and Syriacs. This had devastating consequences

---

[10] Georges-Joseph Mahfoud, *L'organisation monastique dans l'Église Maronite* (Beyrouth: Bibliothèque de l'Université Saint-Esprit, 1967), 80-91.

[11] Asterios Argyriou, "Christianity in the First Ottoman Era," in *Christianity: A History in the Middle East*, 607-608.

[12] Constantin A. Pachenko, *Arab Orthodox Christians under the Ottomans: 1516-1831* (Jordanville, NY: Holy Trinity Seminary Press), 172-225.

[13] Salim Daccache, "Catholic Missions in the Middle East," in *Christianity: A History in the Middle East*, 691-696.

for monastic life in Asia Minor, where many monasteries were ravished. But despite these setbacks, and partially as a response to them, a renewal of monastic life throughout the region was imminent.

The Renewal of Monastic Life and Mission in the 20th Century

Perhaps the renewal of monastic life in Egypt is most widely known and well documented. Its chief sources were the renewal of Christian education through the Sunday School Movement and the involvement of young, well-educated lay people in the Coptic Church, many of whom took monastic vows in the mid-20th century. Prior to that, about seven Coptic monasteries were inhabited by a handful of monks only. Today, there are around 50 monasteries and thousands of monks.[14] The reform prioritized the celebration of the Eucharist and the study of theology, restoring them to the heart of monastic life. Spiritual disciplines were practised with new fervour and theological depth. Monasteries also opened their doors to groups of believers who came on pilgrimages or retreats. In this way, the spiritual and theological revival spread from the monasteries to the parishes of the Coptic Church.[15] An especially missionary role was played by communities of Coptic women, some of which were commissioned to active service in education and medical work.[16]

The Greek Orthodox Patriarchate of Antioch and All the East also saw a renewal of its monastic life in the second half of the 20th century. Some monasteries and convents were restored and inhabited anew by monks and nuns. Other functioning houses were renovated and their communities strengthened.[17] In the Syriac Orthodox community, monasteries also become more prominent, especially the Mor Gabriel monastery in the Tur Abdin region in southeast Anatolia, which suffered persecution during World War I and from which most of the Syriac population emigrated in the course of the 20th century. This monastery played a symbolic and nostalgic role for many emigres, who visited it during the summer and reunited with friends and relatives. Other Syriac Orthodox monasteries in the region fulfilled a similar role within this transnational community. Monks helped socialize the young members into the faith community. In recent years, some nuns have claimed a role in theological education and the service of displaced people.[18] Other communities experienced similar monastic renewals and three cases are considered in more detail here: the

---

[14] Katja Dorothea Buck, "New life behind high walls: Egypt's monasteries bursting at the seams," accessed 5 January 2024, www.oikoumene.org, 12 December 2017.

[15] Catherine Mayeur-Jaouen, "The Coptic Mouleds: Evolution of the Traditional Pilgrimages," in Nelly van Doorn-Harder and Kari Vogt, eds., *Between the Desert and the City: The Coptic Orthodox Church Today* (Eugene, OR: Wipf and Stock, 1997), 213-229.

[16] Nelly van Doorn-Harder, "Discovering New Roles: Coptic Nuns and Church Revival," in *Between the Desert and the City*, 83-98.

[17] Poujeau, "Monastic Movements and Spirituality," 395.

[18] Heleen Murre-van den Berg, "De Syrisch-orthodoxe Kerk," in *Handboek Oosters Christendom*, 170-171.

Armenian Apostolic Church, the Maronite Church, and the Greek Catholic Church.

Several historical factors may have contributed to the renewal of monastic life and its missionary engagement in the 20th century. In the case of Coptic Christianity, scholars agree that the Sunday School Movement and the ensuing monastic reforms were a response to Protestant mission in Egypt. The end of the Ottoman Empire, the formation of new nation states, and the rising nationalism and self-awareness in Middle Eastern Christian communities may also have contributed to the reclamation of monasteries, especially in those communities that experienced persecution and massacres. In addition to these external factors, the rediscovery and recovery of the ancient tradition of monasticism, centred around the spiritual power of holy men and women, and its pivotal role in ecclesial life appears to be a decisive factor in all traditions and may account for the growing numbers of vocations in the second half of the 20th century.

Armenian Monasticism: Mission and the Survival of the Community

We now turn to a more detailed consideration of missionary aspects of Armenian, Maronite and Greek Catholic monasticism in the 20th century. We begin with Armenian monasticism. Much like the pattern elsewhere in the region, Armenian monasticism began with a proto-anchorite movement of monks who sought solitude in the forests and deserts but also preached the gospel in the cities. Many of them were martyred. In the 4th and 5th centuries, the christianization of Armenia coincided with the rise of monasticism throughout the Middle East and Armenian monasticism developed with influences from Cappadocia and Syria.[19] Gregory the Illuminator brought monks and preachers from Cappadocia and thereby stimulated monastic life. According to tradition, Gregory founded the famous monastery of Mush to house relics of apostles. Mush remained a main centre of spirituality, education, science, economics, and military development in the Middle Ages and early modern period.[20]

In the early centuries, Armenian monks contributed to the evangelization of parts of Asia Minor and the Caucasus regions. In the Middle Ages, between the weakening of the Abbasid central rule and the invasion of the Seljuks, Armenia enjoyed relative peace and self-determination, and various monasteries were established and re-established. While there is evidence of Armenian nunneries in the 4th and the 5th centuries, especially during the patriarchate of Nerses the Great and his heir Sahak – the golden age – they appear to have been discontinued in the Middle Ages. In the Middle Ages and the early modern period, the monasteries were centres of learning, development, agriculture, and business. This was the case where Armenians formed a majority of the population but also where they were a minority. In New Julfa, Isfahan, for example, the convent of St Catharine was founded in 1623 and remained

[19] Jean Mécérian, *Histoire et institutions de l'Église arménienne: Evolution nationale et doctrinale, spiritualité, monachisme* (Beyrouth: Dar el Marchreq, 1998), 205-212.

[20] Archbishop Shnorhk Kalsdian, *Hayzki Sourper* [*Saints of the Armenians*] Third Edition (Tehran: Printing House of the Prelacy. 2001), 172.

operational until 1954, with a girls' school attached to it.[21] There was often a close connection between Armenian nobles and the monasteries. Monastic life was also closely linked to the hierarchy of the Armenian Apostolic Church and centred around the seats of the patriarchs.

Out of the work of the western Catholic missionaries emerged a large monastic movement that sought unification with Rome during and the Middle Ages- the Mekhitarist Order (1701) with houses in the Middle East and Europe; its most famous house was located on the Isle of St Lazarus in Venice. Some branches of this order were actively involved in evangelism among Armenians outside the Middle East.[22] While monasticism went through periods of great suffering and bloom, the general image of Armenian monastic life, both Orthodox and Catholic, prior to the Genocide is one of a steady spiritual and cultural influence on the Armenian nation.

The catastrophic events of the Hamidian Massacres (1894-1896) and the Armenian Genocide (1915-1921) drastically changed the mission of Armenian monasticism. In Anatolia, no Armenian monastery remained intact and many monks and priests perished. The monastery of Mush was sacked and, later in the 20th century, razed to the ground. Its loss was symbolic of the harm done to the Armenian community in Asia Minor. Many other ancient monasteries of Cilicia suffered the same fate. In the wake of the Genocide, humanitarian work became the highest priority in displaced Armenian communities. Many survivors were housed in camps in cities like Aleppo and Beirut, and the surviving priests and monks became involved in providing shelter, education, income generation, trauma healing, and spiritual care. At this time, Armenian monks and priests often collaborated with Protestant and Catholic agencies in relief work, which led to a reduction of the antagonism between the ecclesial families.

In the Soviet Republic of Armenia, the church found itself also in a kind of exile, for it faced serious opposition and restrictions. Monasteries were dispossessed and Catholicos Khoren Muradpegian was assassinated by the Soviet authorities in 1938.[23] The only Armenian monastery that continued to function, besides the already mentioned convent of St Catharine and St Makarios Monastery (Magaravank) in Cyprus, was St James in Jerusalem, where some Cilician monks found shelter and considered what their new mission could be.[24] In Constantinople, a handful of monks continued to run the Patriarchate in the absence of a Patriarch and under much pressure from the Turkish government.

The Genocide and the Bolshevik Revolutions were followed by a time of slow healing and recovery. In 1930, Catholicos Sahak II moved the Catholicosate from Sis in Cilicia to Antelias, on the Lebanese shore. The land was donated by

---

[21] Abel Oghlukian, *The Deaconess in the Armenian Church: A Brief Survey* (New Rochelle, NY: St Nersess Armenian Seminary, 1994), 29.

[22] John Whooley, "The Mekhitarists: Religion, Culture, and Ecumenism in Armenian-Catholic Relations," in *Eastern Christianity: Studies in Modern History, Religion and Politics*, ed. Anthony O'Mahony (London: Melisende, 2004), 452-489.

[23] Felix Corley, "The Armenian Church under the Soviet Regime, Part 1: The Leadership of Kevork," *Religion, State, & Society* 24/1 (1996), 9-11.

[24] Puzant Yeghiayan, *Contemporary History of the Catholicosate of the Armenians of Cilicia 1914-1972* (Antelias: Catholicosate of Cilicia, 1975), 90.

the Near East Relief, an American aid organization that had run an orphanage for Armenian survivors in that location in the 1920s. It became the site of the new Catholicosate, a monastery, and a seminary to train priests. Ever since, the Order of the Great House of Cilicia has played a pivotal role in the Armenian Apostolic Church in the diaspora. It became a centre of Armenian religious and cultural life and guaranteed a steady flow of well-trained new priests and monks who ministered and taught in the parishes and church-affiliated schools. These priests and monks helped diaspora communities preserve the faith and the Armenian language and culture. This identity-preserving mission was conducted in ethnically and religiously diverse societies, and as a result the Catholicosate of Cilicia developed in a more ecumenical direction globally due its presence in all continents.[25]

In Soviet Armenia, the church was given some space to manoeuvre after the death of Stalin in 1953. Under Catholicos Vazgen I, several historic churches and monasteries were restored. However, the church was mostly limited to a role of cultural monument and could not engage in a mission of spirituality and Christian education.[26] A true revival of monasticism occurred after the fall of the Soviet Union and the independence of the Republic of Armenia in 1991. Monasteries were reoccupied and monks endeavoured to transform them into centres of spirituality rather than mere historic monuments. Pilgrims from inside and outside the country flocked once again to the tombs of saints such as St Hripsime and St Gregory of Datev. The women's order of St Hripsime was reconstituted albeit on a very modest scale. At this time, monks had a baptismal mission, making 'the first Christian nation' Christian again, after years of state-promoted atheism. The monks also contributed to the reorganization of the church in the new republic and to Christian education through the establishment of educational centres. The aim of such educational efforts was to restore the doctrinal and ethical teaching of the Armenian Apostolic Orthodox Church to the heart of the nation, but persistent political corruption and socio-economic inequalities were evidence that the church was unable to recover its central position and provide the moral guidance that it believed was needed.[27]

Maronite Monasticism: Witness and Service

The Maronite Church has rightly been called a monastic community, for it traces its origins back to the 4th century ascetic Maron, who lived in northern Syria and

---

[25] S. Peter Cowe, "Church and diaspora: the case of the Armenians," in *The Cambridge History of Christianity, Part III: Eastern Christianity*, ed. Michael Angold (Cambridge: Cambridge University Press, 2006), 430-456. Catholicos Aram I, *Facing New Horizons* (Antelias: Armenian Catholicosate of Cilicia, 2018).

[26] Hratch Tchilingirian, "In Search of Relevance: Church and Religion in Armenia since Independence," in *Religion et politique dans le Caucase post-soviétique: Les traditions réinventées à l'épreuve des influences extérieures*, ed. Bayram Balci and Raoul Motika (Institut français d'études Anatoliennes, 2007), 277-311.

[27] Hratch Tchilingirian, "Armenia and Karabakh," in *Christianity in North Africa and West Asia*, 195.

whose followers formed a monastic community in Apamea, Syria, and on the banks of the Orontes River in Lebanon. Over the centuries, the community grew and the appointment of its own patriarch in the 8th century may be viewed as the beginning of the Maronite Church. Pushed by confessional and religious persecutions, the Maronites concentrated their presence in the northern part of Lebanon, a safer place against conquerors. The Maronite patriarchs established themselves in Yanouh then in Mayfouq, the two villages located in the Lebanese region of Batroun-Byblos, before they moved their seat to the inaccessible Qadisha Valley, which became a major centre of Maronite monastic life. The Maronites then gradually moved southwards and monks played an important role in the settlement and christianization of the central Lebanese mountain range.[28]

Hence, Pope John Paul II words in *Orientale Lumen* "Monasticism has always been the very soul of the Eastern Churches"[29] are particularly true for the Maronite Church. Echoing this papal assertion, the Patriarchal Synod of this church (2003-2006) recognized that "monastic life constituted the nerve of Maronite ecclesiastical life… and this role remained active throughout history until the present day."[30] In other words, without monasticism that accompanied her birth and made her flourish, the Maronite Church "would not have been herself."[31] Therefore, it is interesting to see how Maronite monks and nuns, although characterized by their austere and ascetic way of life, have always been intensely involved in the mission of the church.[32] Statistical data give an idea of

[28] For more information see: Butros Daou, *History of the Maronites: Religious, Cultural and Political* (Beirut [no publisher] 1984), 558-561. Herman Teule, "De Maronitische Kerk," in *Handboek Oosters Christendom*, 187-196.

[29] Pope John Paul II, Apostolic Letter Orientale Lumen (May 2, 1995), 9.

[30] *Maronite Patriarchal Synod, 2003-2006: Texts & Recommendations* (Bkerké: Maronite Patriarchate of Antioch and the Entire East, 2008). Text 8: Monasticism in the Maronite Church, 4.

[31] *Maronite Patriarchal Synod*, Text 8.1 (p. 283). A leading monastic scholar wrote: "It is a unique phenomenon in the history of the Universal Church, where we know of no other Church that originated from a monastery and became pivoted around it, despite what monastic movements had a profound influence on the life of the Churches in the East and the West. It is therefore perfectly natural for the Church of the Maronites to be distinguished through a heremitic and monastic spirituality imprinted in her since her inception, and her history became entwined with the fate of monastic life which became tantamount to being a throbbing heart within her." Elias Khalifeh, "The Church of Maronites and its relation with monastic life," *Monastic Journal* 47 (1995), 86.

[32] This double characteristic contemplative-apostolic monastic life goes back to the dawn of the Antiochene Syriac tradition, starting with the fourth century, as it is pointed out by the Maronite Patriarchal Synod: "The Antiochene Syriac monastic life during this stage [4th-7th c.] was distinguished by utter austerity and the living of various heremitic patterns and was also characterized by undertaking preaching, evangelization and mission activities. Writers testify that the monks of the Saint Maron Monastery were not limiting their activities to hermitages, perfection through virtue and the saving of their souls, but pursued the apostolic mission, giving due regard to the saving of the souls of others also. Nuns played a supporting role and mother superiors of convents were charged with the diaconal task of anointing with oil the women candidates for baptism after their foreheads were anointed by the priest. The Christian faith did not encompass all of Syria and Mesopotamia and did not spread in the regions of Persia, Armenia and

the extent of this role in the church's mission and the observation of the various aspects of their activities shows the powerful correlation of the Maronite monastic life with that of the people of God.

While Maronite monastic life had been uninterrupted, it received a major impulse during its reform in the year 1695.[33] Later, in the 20th century, Maronite monasticism shared in the monastic revival in the region with an increase in the number of vocations and an expansion of the monasteries. In the first decade of the 21st century, members of the Maronite orders numbered 1,543: 723 monks and 820 nuns.[34] It is a significant number for a country of roughly four million inhabitants distributed among 18 religions and denominations.

There are four religious congregations for men based in Lebanon.[35] The Lebanese Maronite Order and the Maronite Order of the Blessed Virgin Mary derive both from the first Order which organized monastic life starting in 1695, before it was split in 1770. The Antonine Order was founded in 1700, purposely in a non-Christian environment and grew particularly in completely non-Christian areas of Lebanon. In the middle of the 19th century, a congregation dedicated to mission was launched. In fact, the Congregation of Maronite Lebanese Missionaries, whose statutes were approved by the Maronite Patriarch in 1873, embraced the mission of evangelization through preaching of the word, spiritual direction, the media, writing and education.

Beside a couple of eparchial monasteries, there are five active religious congregations for women. Two of them, the Maronite Lebanese Nuns and the Maronite Antonine Nuns, were linked to the corresponding aforementioned male Orders until the middle of the last century. The other three were established especially for mission. The Society of the Maronite Sisters of the Holy Family started in 1895 as a monastic missionary congregation dedicated to the educational, social, and pastoral service of the family and catechetical Christian formation. Similarly, the Society of the Maronite Sisters of Saint Therese of the Child Jesus was established in 1935 with the main goal of serving orphanages, hospitals and shelters. Finally, the Society of the Missionary Nuns of the Blessed Sacrament was founded more recently, in 1966, to propagate the devotion to the Blessed Sacrament but also to provide formation for village girls and to assist parish priests in their various apostolic activities under the motto: "Send me to announce glad tidings to the poor and to heal the broken hearted" (Luke 4:18).

India, except through the great apostolic activity undertaken by the Syriac monks through steadfastness and faith." *Maronite Patriarchal Synod* 8.3 (p. 286).

[33] Inspired by the western orders that were present in the region—the Capuchins, Franciscans, Carmeltes, and Jesuits—the hitherto autonomous monasteries were organized into a single order. For a detailed discussion of the 1695 reform, see: Georges-Joseph Mahfoud, *L'organisation monastique dans l'Église maronite: Étude historique* (Kaslik: Bibliothèque de l'Université Saint-Esprit, 1967), 129-157.

[34] *Maronite Patriarchal Synod* 8.1.

[35] In the late 1980s, a Maronite religious community was founded in Petersham, Massachusetts, under the name of the Most Holy Trinity Monastery. This eparchial congregation established a satellite monastery in Nova Scotia in the year 2000.

Whether they are specifically missionaries or not, all these religious congregations are deeply involved in the mission of the church. Their apostolic activity, sometimes within the same institution, has many aspects. In its document about monasticism, the Maronite Patriarchal Synod reserves one chapter for "The Mission of the Monastic Institutions" where these activities are categorized into five fields. Very significantly, witness comes top of the list. As witness is, in our opinion, the chief characteristic of Maronite monasticism, we will discuss it more elaborately after a quick overview of the other four areas of activity: education, development, pastoral, and social involvement.

Education is without doubt the most prominent role played by the monastic institutions in Lebanon where, at present, approximately 70 percent of the student body are enrolled in private schools. This reality has a historical background. In the previous three centuries, only monks and some educated parish priests could provide basic education for young people in the villages of Mount Lebanon, whereas foreign Catholic missions established their schools in the cities.[36] Moreover, the rivalry between Catholic and Protestant missions provoked a missionary expansion beginning in 1830 and urged the Maronites to reinforce their educational activities.[37] Until now, the deeply rooted confessional political system of the country makes each community keen to have its own educational institutions and adds to the deficiency of the public educational sector. Maronite monks and nuns are currently running about 100 prominent schools, 20 technical and vocational institutes and four universities. One of these universities hosts the only Pontifical Faculty of Theology in the East, where the majority of the ministers of the Catholic churches receive their philosophical and theological formation. Generously funded by monastic orders, these institutions provide higher education for young people coming from various religious denominations. They offer curricula in multiple sectors and at international standards (some enjoy international accreditation). They also contribute to the preservation of the cultural heritage of the church: liturgical, linguistic, musical, artistic, etc.

When they spoke about mission on the level of development, the Fathers of the Patriarchal Synod intended mainly the contribution of monastic orders to the agricultural sector, which is very important for the Maronites. In reality, cultivating the land is not merely an economic matter. The land is sacred in the spirituality of this community, which often found refuge in mountains and valleys. It is the link between the present and the previous generations who endured all kinds of sacrifices to preserve it. Mount Lebanon is known in history

---

[36] Abbot Paul Naaman recounts how his monastic congregation decided, after World War I, to develop its already existent schools in remote areas, Notre Dame of Mashmousheh in the South and Notre Dame of Mayfouq in the region of Jbeil. "The evolution of the view of education in the Lebanese Maronite Order; Part 1: From 1695 to 1737; and Part II: From 1920 to 1950," *The Tricentenary of the Lebanese Maronite Order: History and Future Prospects, 1695-1995* (Kaslik: Publications of the Institute of History at the Holy Spirit University of Kaslik, 1996), 383-417.

[37] The history of the missions in the Middle East, namely in Lebanon, is well presented by Fr. Salim Daccache, "Catholic Missions in the Middle East," in *Christianity. A History in the Middle East*, 687-710.

as a space of freedom and a safe shelter for oppressed people, in a surrounding area of recurrent conquests and a persistent atmosphere of religious intolerance. Their hard labour and their mastery in land exploitation allowed monks not only to maintain the presence of Christians in Lebanon but also to foster their expansion across the country. Thanks to a system of partnership with the people living in the areas nearby,[38] the monks 'extended' the limits of their monasteries, since "these people were to participate in the cultivation of the land and to revive the Divine Office and spiritual exchange, thus forming the greater family of the monastery."[39]

The pastoral service rendered by the Catholic monastic institutions to the church in Lebanon was so vast that it received the praise of John Paul II: "Religious communities are a great treasure and a source of grace and dynamism for the dioceses. Through their various apostolic activities, they participate in the pastoral work led by the bishops and, as a result, are integrated into the various diocesan bodies."[40] With a sense of pride and gratitude, the Maronite Synod enumerates those activities, within parishes and beyond.

> The monks assisted by the nuns ensure service to parishes close to their monasteries as well as those distant from it, in and outside Lebanon. They care for the sick in 13 hospitals which they run. They also provide preaching, spiritual retreats, confessions, guidance in schools, universities, prisons and hospitals. They establish orphanages, homes for the elderly and the handicapped. They contribute through invigorating the university pastoral work and the judicial, media, and social apostolate as well as other ecclesiastical fields they might be asked to participate in or even to be charged with its responsibility. Moreover, monastic orders foster and guide cultural, apostolic and scout movements and others.[41]

The social mission of Maronite monks and nuns is carried out under the motif of solidarity. They have a keen awareness of being of the people and for the people. "Their monasteries were known as a refuge for the needy as they opened wide their monasteries and centres, transforming them into refuges and restaurants for the wretched during World War II and the last Lebanese war (1975-1990)."[42] In times of crisis, they strive to help the needy wherever possible, through their educational, social and services institutions. Recently, a number of congregations have undertaken the construction of apartments to offer to young families with payment facilities in order to keep them in the country.

Above all these apostolic activities, the evangelical witness of life is the greatest mission monastic orders provide to the Maronite Church. This type of mission reverses the direction of movement in the apostolate. While missionaries are normally sent (*missus*) to people, in the case of authentic monastic mission it is rather the people who come to the monasteries. These places obviously offer a serene atmosphere of peace that many people seek in a permanently anxious

---

[38] According to this system, lay people exploit the land and receive a part, usually half, of the harvest.

[39] *Maronite Patriarchal Synod* 8.38, 309-310.

[40] John Paul II, Apostolic Exhortation 'A New Hope for Lebanon,' 10 May 1997, 54.

[41] *Maronite Patriarchal Synod* 8.39, 310-311.

[42] Ibid. 8.40, 311.

world. But on a religious level, further reasons could explain this attraction, among them the sacramental tradition including the celebration of the Divine Liturgy and the fascination with the consecrated life. In this sense, the Maronite Synod recalls that "of the most important fruits of monastic life is the abundance of graces poured forth as a result of the regular prayers raised in most of the monasteries and hermitages."[43] This spiritual radiance is particularly manifest in monasteries where monks or nuns were distinguished by their heroic virtues. "The last century and the beginning of this century were marked by the glitter of the era of the beatification and canonization of some monks and nuns. The holiness of Father Sharbel Makhlouf, and the nun Rafka ar-Rayes and recently Father Neemetallah Kassab al-Hardini was declared. Their fame and their Maronite monastic approach spread throughout the world."[44] Their tombs have become sanctuaries attracting Christian and non-Christian visitors alike from Lebanon, the Arabian region and the world. In fact, authentic monastic mission crosses over religious boundaries and geographical borders.

In this regard, it is worth mentioning the phenomenon of the 22nd of each month in Annaya, the sanctuary of Saint Sharbel in Lebanon, and in almost every Maronite centre across the world. Thousands of people gather to see and hear, again and again, the testimony of Nohad Chamy. This Lebanese mother of 12 children was suffering from hemiplegia when, on 22 January 1993, Saint Sharbel miraculously healed her by performing a surgery on her neck, then asking her to visit his hermitage every 22nd day of the month, and attend mass for the rest of her life. This marvel continues until today and is spreading. People from every denomination and at times from different religions gather for an intense moment of spiritual blessing. The monthly pilgrimage has indeed become an ecumenical mission. For many, it also realizes what Jesus calls for, beyond the healing of the body, the conversion of heart.

Greek Catholic (Melkite) Monasticism: Mission with Tongue and Plume[45]

While monasticism had been part of the Greek Catholic tradition from its beginnings in the 17th century, the 20th century saw the rise of a distinctly missionary order within this Uniate tradition. The Society of the Missionaries of Saint Paul was founded in Harissa (Lebanon) in 1903 by Germanos Mu'aqqad, a Syrian bishop of the Melkite Catholic Church. During his episcopal ministry in Baalbeck (1886-1894), Mu'aqqad felt called to engage with the faithful who were ignorant in matters of faith. At that time, many members of the clergy were

---

[43] Ibid. 8.36, 308-309.

[44] Ibid. 8.36.

[45] This section relies on the following publications: Philippe Gorra, *La société des Missionnaires grecs-catholiques de Saint Paul Harissa,Liban* (Cairo: Ed. Edouard Hakim, 1935); Wissam B. Kabkab, *The Society of the Missionaries of Saint Paul: Foundation - Organization - Mission, vol. 1 1903-1951* (Jounieh: Library of Saint Paul, 1987) (in Arabic); *La Société des Missionnaires de Saint Paul. Année du 1er Centenaire de sa fondation (1903-2003)*- a booklet published in Arabic and French at the occasion of the centenary of the Society.

profoundly under-educated, not only in his diocese, located in a relatively remote region, but in the entire Levant. This grave reality alerted him to the urgent need for the church to have missionary priests. Mu'aqqad had previously been at the Seminary of St Anne, which he had founded in Jerusalem in collaboration with the Missionaries of Africa (the White Fathers) in 1881. With this experience in mind, he resigned as bishop and decided to establish a community of priests, including coadjutor brothers, devoted uniquely to the mission. During his short stay in Rome (1896) where he obtained the benediction of Pope Leo XIII for his project, he visited the basilica of St Paul Outside the Walls. In this sanctuary he was inspired to dedicate his future society to the Apostle to the Gentiles.

The purpose of the society was clearly defined in a patriarchal authorization decree and was included in the founding constitution. The Missionaries of St Paul were not to be parish ministers; they were even specifically prohibited to carry on pastoral activities. It was for this reason that Mu'aqqad decided to establish the society in the district of Kesrwan in Mount Lebanon where no Melkite parish existed. Furthermore, the chosen location in Harissa, near the sanctuary of Our Lady of Lebanon, was at that time a quiet place with an atmosphere favouring contemplation and study. The aim of the new society was to foster the faith and spiritual life of Christians in the Middle East, through the most specific forms of apostolic labour, namely preaching and publishing. "Mission with tongue and plume" became the motto of the society. Later on, Christian unity and the interreligious dialogue also became part of the society's mandate, particularly through research but also in a remarkably visible way in the construction of the basilica of St Paul in Harissa. This basilica had a distinctly Byzantine architecture and the mosaic of the main apse presented the principal representatives of the Catholic and Orthodox Churches side by side, against the background of the cultures of East and West. The mission with tongue was carried out by preaching in parishes; the mission with plume was accomplished through the writing, editing, and printing of Christian literature.

From the outset, the Paulists made it their goal to be "sowers of the Word and builders of souls." They headed to towns and villages, especially in remote areas, in Syria, Lebanon, Jordan and Palestine to achieve that objective. Practically, the mission consisted of preaching and organising spiritual retreats for parishioners as well as for church ministers. Their traditional missionary approach also included liturgical celebrations, religious teachings, confessions, and spiritual counselling. To children and young people, the Paulists offered catechism and training in church music and prayer. Furthermore, they concerned themselves with religious associations for laity, reanimating associations that had been neglected or discontinued as well as creating new ones, especially for women. Beside this strictly speaking spiritual work, the Missionaries of Saint Paul were at times assigned by church hierarchs to administrative duties in the diocesan institutions. Even though the Paulists intended to serve the people of the Levant, from the mid-20th century they were invited to extend their field of mission to the diaspora in North and Latin America, where large numbers of Levantine Christians had moved after the world wars.

In 2003, the Missionaries of Saint Paul celebrated the first centenary of their Society and took stock of their centres of work and mission. In addition to the central house in Harissa, which hosts the seminary and the institute of philosophy and theology, the Missionaries had four centres in Lebanon, among which were the library and the printing press in the city of Jounieh, three centres in Syria, one in Palestine, and two locations in Argentina, Buenos Aires, and Rosario.

Publishing Christian literature occupied a prominent place in the activities of the Society of the Missionaries of Saint Paul. It was indeed a distinctive instrument of their mission, alongside preaching. Driven by the zeal of their founder, the first missionaries began to publish the review *Al Maçarrat* in 1910. It remained the official organ of the Greek Melkite Catholic Patriarchate until 1965. Despite the financial difficulties experienced during the two consecutive world wars and the civil war in Lebanon, this monthly periodical was one of the few journals in the Arab world to exist for more than a century. It covered topics related to the Christian faith and church history. For the purpose of publishing its review, the Society established its own printing press (1910) and later even a professional school (1966-1979) to train people, thus promoting the vocation of printing in the Middle East. Alongside the review, a significant number of other publications (over 500 titles) were edited and diffused, covering multiple areas of studies: biblical, theological, spiritual, philosophical, educational, etc., targeting different categories of readers.

For the education of young people, the Paulists launched a series of educational and school books entitled *Al Mushaweq* ('the attractant'). The series covered books on catechesis, Arabic literature, grammar, history, geography, and the sciences. It met an educational need throughout the 20th century, thus providing effective tools for education in the Arab world. A famous title from the series was Hanna Fakhoury's *History of Arab Philosophy*, which went into several editions and was translated into Russian and Persian. A series of lives of saints entitled *Ash-Shuhud* ('the witnesses') mostly written by Emile Hajj and published since the 1960s, propagated the heroic examples of the great saints of the East and West, making the ideal of holiness accessible to all, especially to young people. Christian literature for younger children was also among the priorities of the Paulists. An illustrated series entitled *Qissas min al-kitab al muqaddas* ('tales from the Holy Bible') was published in 60 volumes, allowing children to take their first steps in knowing God through beautifully illustrated pages.

On the level of theology, the series *Al fikr al masihi bayna al ams wa al yawm* ('Christian thought in past and present') exposed practically all topics of Christian theology, intended for both the general public and specialists. This series, which included Arabic translations of important Catholic ecclesiastical documents, was a useful tool for theology students and pastors as well as lay people seeking a basic theological formation. In the context of interreligious dialogue, the Society launched in the 1950s the series *Nusus cor'aniah* ('Quranic texts'), thus presenting Muslim thought by the pen of a Christian. In the 1990s, this was followed by a series launched by the Center for Study and Research of Islamic-Christian Dialogue (CEDRIC) founded by Adel Theodore Khoury, that presented Christian and Muslim thought side by side.

The Missionary Contributions of the Monastic Orders

Based on our discussion of monasticism in three Middle Eastern Christian traditions, we discern at least three distinctive ways in which the monastic orders contribute to Christian mission as understood in this volume. First, on an elementary level, monastic communities enable Christian presence in the region to continue. As has been demonstrated, monasticism is at the heart of the Christian communities. The monastic communities have a marked closeness to their hierarchies and patriarchs, affirming and strengthening them. From among their ranks, the churches choose teachers, spiritual leaders, and even patriarchs. But monastic communities are also essential to the laity. The usage of monastic lands for agriculture or simply as untouched nature is an ecological mission carried out in cooperation with and for the benefit of local communities. In times of dire need, the monasteries have opened their doors and received uprooted and persecuted people. The very presence of monasteries and convents on the lands provides the Christian communities with geographical centres and bestows a sanctity on the land and its people that is celebrated during pilgrimages to the monasteries. Conversely, the desecration and destruction of monasteries and convents is a symbolic act that aims to discourage Christian presence. This occurred during World War I and more recently at the hands of groups such as ISIS and Al Nusra in Syria and Iraq.

Second, the monastic communities are key players in education in general and Christian education in particular. Through the numerous schools for elementary, secondary, vocational, higher, and special education that they have founded and managed, they have served their own faith communities and other communities from whom pupils were drawn. Monastic communities have also engaged in evangelism and religious education among diaspora communities. Monastic communities offer medical and social services, often making them available to underprivileged segments of the population.

Third, monastic communities fulfil what could be called a cultural mission within the Middle Eastern Christian communities. They preserve, practise, and study the distinctive spiritual, theological, architectural, iconographic, and liturgical traditions of their churches. The ancient liturgical languages (Syriac, Greek, Krapar, Coptic, Assyrian) and arts are appropriated afresh and kept alive in their communal prayers. Many monasteries and convents have been centres of musical and liturgical renewal and innovation. This strengthens the Christian identity of their wider communities.

As our survey shows, there are also areas of tension between the monastic life and missionary engagement. We began by remarking that, to many, monasticism seems to be the very opposite of Christian mission, for the former is marked by withdrawal while the latter is characterized by outreach. Paradoxically, however, it is through withdrawal and contemplation that monks and nuns achieve a holiness that makes them attractive to others. It is not primarily in their activity that monastic communities are missionary, but rather in their very being.

The duality of contemplation and action appears to be alien to Middle Eastern monasticism. In their contemplation they are missionary. For this reason, pilgrimages to monasteries form an important element of the faith of many

Middle Eastern Christians and Muslims. During such visits, the saints to whom the sacred places are dedicated are invoked and the monks and nuns may be consulted and asked for intercession. Anne Poujeau points out that monastic movements today have inherited this role from the ancient holy men and women who took to the desert but were sought out by the multitudes.[46]

Another point of criticism may be the relatively weighty service that the monastic communities render to their own Christian communities and nations (Armenians, Maronites, Syriacs, Copts, etc.) while engaging less frequently with other groups, which may contribute to isolationism. As has been demonstrated, though, through educational and medical initiatives monastic communities have an impact that goes well beyond their own communities. In addition, some communities such as the Paulists have deliberately emphasized ecumenism and interfaith dialogue, thereby strengthening social cohesion and interfaith understanding.

Conclusion

The monastic orders are a formidable missionary presence in Middle Eastern Christianity. Without the monastic movements the churches of the Middle East would probably be more vulnerable and less able to serve their societies. Their presence in these lands is a source of strength and encouragement for the wider Christian communities. As Pope John Paul II wrote, "monasticism has always been the very soul of the Eastern churches."[47] Many of its patriarchs and bishops live in monasteries and help advance the monastic spirituality and dedication among the faithful. The monasteries and convents also help preserve the distinctive spiritualities and theological traditions of the various churches. While monastic communities have at times been part of competition and antagonism between the churches, today, as communities, they exemplify teamwork and cooperation in Christian mission. While the widespread renewal of monasticism in the region in the 20th century appears to have lost some of its momentum at the beginning of the 21st century, numerous monastic communities continue to attract young novices and continue to pray, meditate, write, teach, preach, work the land, and support the vulnerable. Their example continues to inspire many lay people, and there are signs that the 21st century may see an increase in lay organizations that emulate monastic communities in mission and service.

46 Poujeau, "Monastic Movements and Spirituality," 400-401.

47 *Apostolic Letter "Orientale Lumen" of the Supreme Pontiff John Paul II to the Bishops, Clergy and Faithful to Mark the Centenary of Orientale Dignitas of Pope Leo XIII* (2 May 1995), 9.

The Involvement of Protestant Women in Theological Education and Mission in the Middle East from 1921–2021

Grace Al-Zoughbi

Introduction

Her name is unknown in the biblical narrative of John 4. She is referred to only by her ethnicity. However, she becomes the first missionary par excellence, not the first woman missionary but the first missionary. The story takes place in Samaria, 35 kilometres north of Bethlehem, where I was born and raised. In fact, I can well picture the context of this conversation–the geographical setting of Mount Gerizim and Ebal is ideal–high, green, with open air. The context is marred by political complexity, yes, but its unique characteristics burst with theological elements on which to reflect. For several reasons I find the story significant in relation to the mission narrative. First, in John 4, Jesus challenges the patriarchal norms of the society when he initiates a theological conversation with a *Samaritan* and a *woman*. Second, Jesus reveals to the Samaritan woman his divine identity, and profound theological truths. Third, the Samaritan woman recounts her encounter with the Messiah to the whole of Samaria, and many believed in Jesus.

In the Orthodox tradition, the Samaritan woman is referred to as St Photeine. The Passion of Photeine was written between the 6th or 7th centuries and the 10th century.[1] She is commemorated as a martyr who was persecuted with her sisters and sons by the Roman Emperor Nero in Carthage.

Today Arab women in the Middle East continue to be involved in mission in the same place and beyond where the witness and testimony of faith was embodied. Their narratives are a continuation of this legacy. The same Spirit that worked in the lives of biblical women, commissioning them as carriers of the gospel, dwells in the lives of contemporary Arab women. I am one of these Arab women. I have recently completed my doctoral research on the theological education of Arab women in the Middle East. I was particularly impacted by the amount of undocumented mission work accomplished in the Middle East by Arab women. I was startled that these women, like the Samaritan, operate in a culture of honour and shame, but still count it worthy to share the good news regardless of the sacrifices this might entail. They are prepared to go where a man cannot and they consider it an honour to carry the gospel's message.

---

[1] Christine B. Lindner, "Women and Christianity in the Middle East," in *The Rowman and Littlefield Handbook of Christianity in the Middle East*, ed. Mitri Raheb and Mark A. Lamport (Lanham, Boulder, New York, and London: Rowman & Littlefield, 2020), 398- 413, citing 499.

Therefore, a look at the Egyptian and Syrian mission context is fitting for the purposes of this contribution. However, these accounts are more than history; they invite us to reflect on how the contemporary debates are framed. Looking at the trajectory of scholarship which has made a significant contribution, has influenced how I understand the contemporary situation. In dealing with a highly complex confluence of historical influences, different scholars have responded in a variety of ways to the context. My quest is to be authoritative in understanding and presenting the historical narrative which has contextualized Protestant missions in the Middle East. Some scholars write from the outside and may not always be cognisant of the cultural and ecclesial dynamic on which they are commenting. As an insider researcher, I have the opportunity of extending the debate. Having built on some of the helpful insights of other scholars, I have repositioned the narrative around Arab women, giving them a voice, since Arab Protestant Women's (APW) voices are seldom present in the narrative.

Definition of Mission

Pamela Chrabieh draws our attention to the fact that despite the numerous remarkable studies that have been published in the last two to three decades, little has been written on contemporary Arab Christian women.[2] In situating my research as a contribution to knowledge on APW in theological education, which is a significantly under-researched field of study, I include theological education in my definition of mission. I posit that there is value in ensuring that women have access to missional theological education. APW can be catalysts in various ways within their ecclesial and theological academic settings, including through their contributions to theological education. A focus on women's education has supported the widening of the role of women in ministry within Protestant communities in the Middle East.[3] Building on a body of literature in the modern history of the Protestant missions in the Middle East, my contribution is to reflect on Protestant women in the Middle East in theological education. My research led me to spend considerable time in the field intentionally considering APW in theological education. In studying the lived realities of Arab women in theological education, I became acquainted with the narratives of Arab women within their intensely ecclesial and missional context.

Much of the theological education in the Middle East was established as a result of the efforts of Western missions, both Catholic and Protestant. The great expansion of Protestant missions in the 19th century saw missionaries travelling to the Middle East, Africa, India and to other parts of Asia. Protestant Christianity did not thrive in the Middle East as it did in Africa. Nevertheless, mature Protestant churches have developed and are active in their communities,

---

[2] Pamela Chrabieh, "Women in Middle Eastern Christianity," in *Surviving Jewel: The Enduring Story of Christianity in the Middle East*, ed. Mitri Raheb and Mark A. Lamport (Eugene, OR: Cascade Books, 2022), 199.

[3] David Grafton, "Protestants," in *The Rowman & Littlefield Handbook of Christianity in the Middle East*, 319.

although they are still a minority[4] among the Christian denominations in the Middle East. The expansion of Christian missions to the lands stretching from Morocco to Iran and from Turkey to Yemen has experienced a flourishing in recent years. Further, historiography has made a distinction between "home missions," for the purpose of strengthening local communities and "foreign missions," with the focus of converting non-Christians. This distinction, however, is inapplicable to the Middle East missions, where the Christian communities go back to the origin of Christianity. As Chantal Verdeil suggests: "They belonged to societies dominated by Islam, which prohibited conversion. Other religious groups, Jews or communities that were offshoots of Islam, such as the Alawites or Druze, offered greater hope (of conversion), which usually went unfulfilled."[5] 'In the Middle East, the missions primarily targeted Christians, like the "home missions," but remained "foreign" until the onset of decolonization blurred the distinction."[6]

In drawing on the Egyptian and Syrian context of missions, I intend to bring out some of the distinctiveness of the contribution of Arab women. I will start with the Egyptian context.

The Egyptian Missionary Context

The Protestant presence in Egypt goes back to the mid-19th century, when missionaries from the American United Presbyterian Mission arrived. In 1854, the Presbyterian Church of Egypt built the first school for girls in Egypt at a time when it was considered inappropriate to educate girls. Subsequently, Christian and Muslim girls, even those living in the isolated villages, completed at least six years of primary education.[7] This fact, however, is not to imply a typical Western gaze towards the East–that the West was the first to initiate the concept of education in the Middle East–or to suggest that the indigenous church, the Coptic Orthodox Church, was not encouraging girls' education. I came to realize through my research that Pope Cyril IV (1854-1861) built the first school for girls in Egypt.[8]

---

[4] Many Copts do not see themselves as a minority and would consider this an inaccurate description of their status. For them, "minority" indicates weakness and detracts from their authenticity. Mariz Tadros suggests, "[t]o speak of Christian minorities, in particular, with respect to the Middle Eastern countries … is not without its problems." Mariz Tadros, "Christianity in North Africa and West Asia," in *Christianity in North Africa and West Asia*, ed. Kenneth R. Ross, Mariz Tadros and Todd M. Johnson (Edinburgh: Edinburgh University Press, 2018), 17-18.

[5] Chantal Verdeil, "Mission Movements to and from the Middle East," in *The Rowman & Littlefield Handbook of Christianity in the Middle East*, 99-109 citing 99.

[6] Ibid., 99-109 citing 99.

[7] Anne Zaki, "Against the Current: Rethinking Gender, Religious Authority and Interreligious Dialogues" in *Middle Eastern Women: The Intersection of Law, Culture and Religion*, ed. Mitrī Rāḥib (Bethlehem: Diyar Publisher, 2020), 218.

[8] Lois M Farag, "Beyond their Gender: Contemporary Coptic Female Monasticism Source," *Journal of World Christianity* 2:1 (2009), 111– 144 citing 124.

One hundred years later, in 1954, Presbyterians established two schools for female evangelists in Menia and Tanta. In 1970 the Evangelical Theological Seminary in Cairo (ETSC) had its first female graduate, Victoria Aziz Fahim, and women have been completing theological degrees there since then.[9] The Evangelical Presbyterian Church of Egypt has 250,000 members, 234 pastors, and 314 congregations.[10] Many women who have received theological education serve within these congregations.

Women and Theological Education

The commitment of the church in Egypt to theological education dates back to the early days of Christianity when Egypt offered the Christian world its first structured theological education.[11] Not only did theological learning at an institutional level start in Alexandria, but Egypt was also a prominent centre for the spread of Christianity with outstanding missionary activities. While theology is simply a discourse about θεός (God) and subjects related to God, theological education is the domain of educating and training those involved in this discourse. Theological education implies educators, learners, administrators, and a situational context, whether formal or non-formal, for education to take place. Activities of theological education include doing theology (the prescriptive step by step processes of engaging in theological reflection to produce a theological work), studying, learning, and thinking about the scriptures, learning biblical languages, cultural contexts, and non-formal theological education. The church and academy are included in my definition of theological education. Whilst the focus here is on formal theological education, my discussion includes some aspects of non-formal theological education.

The "surge" in Middle Eastern seminaries is well documented by Jayson Casper.[12] In Egypt, this surge is partly due to its vast population. It can also be attributed to the commitment of Christians to pursue theological education regardless of their professional background.[13] Today ETSC alumni form the largest Protestant community in ministry in the Middle East. They have served throughout most of the countries in the Middle East and North Africa. Given the high rate of emigration, graduates are also serving the Protestant Arab diaspora in Australia, Canada, England, Germany, and the United States. In 2006, ETSC established a Centre for Middle Eastern Christianity. Scholars from other Christian traditions have been invited here to give lectures, thus making space for ecumenical dialogue.[14]

---

[9] Zaki, "Against the Current," 219.

[10] "Evangelical Presbyterian Church of Egypt Synod of the Nile," World Council of Churches, accessed 1 January 2023, https://www.oikoumene.org/member-churches/Evangelical-presbyterian-church-of-egypt-synod-of-the-nile.

[11] Wafik Wahba, "Coptic Christians," in *The Rowman & Littlefield Handbook of Christianity in the Middle East*, 228.

[12] Jayson Casper, "The Surge in Arab Seminary Studies," *Christianity Today*, 9 July 2022, accessed 30 May 2013, https://jaysoncasper.com/2022/07/09/the-surge-in-arab-seminary-studies/.

[13] Wahba, "Coptic Christians," 229.

[14] Grafton, "Protestants," 319.

There are various works on the roles that Western women played in Arab churches as missionaries and teachers, who also helped to shape some of the cultural and social barriers while opening up others. Viewing these in light of discussions about Muslim Arab women and religious education is part of the general context in the Middle East. Roded wrote about Muslim female theologians.[15] The literature on Palestinian women tends to focus on the political and less on people's social and cultural lives. Greenberg gives some historical background to the social and cultural reasons why Palestinian girls were not able to study.[16] Rubenberg discusses many barriers and, of course, the issue of patriarchy.[17] There are various resources on women, gender, and patriarchy in Egypt; most deal with the 1920s and 1930s.[18] Sharkey focused on education and missions in Sudan and Egypt.[19]

Catherine Mayeur-Jaouen studied the interweaving of missionary activities and social work involving both nuns and laywomen in Egypt from the 1940s to the 1970s. Drawing on case studies mainly in Upper Egypt, she shows that the development of female missionary actions resulted from male initiatives in regions displaying major social disparities. She highlights the growing and central role of lay men and women within the religious domain.[20] Hence, I would like to call attention to two Egyptian women who served in the missional aspect of theological education in a lay capacity, albeit from a Protestant tradition. Learning about their lives reveals the unique aspects women in mission can bring to strengthen the importance of relevant missional theological education for women.

Mathilde Binyameen Sawerus: Education Pioneer in Assiut.[21]

Western missionaries chose Mathilde Binyameen Sawerus to become the first Egyptian principal for the girls' academy in Assiut (where currently two Synod schools operate: the Developed School of Peace and the School of Peace for Languages). Matilde was born in 1923 to a family from Assiut known for their faith and love of the church and homeland. She was raised in a family of four

[15] Ruth Roded, ed., *Women in Islam and the Middle East: A Reader*, revised edition (London: I.B. Tauris, 2008).

[16] Ela Greenberg, *Preparing the Mothers of Tomorrow: Education and Islam in Mandate Palestine* (Austin, Tex: University of Texas Press, 2010).

[17] Cheryl Rubenberg, *Palestinian Women: Patriarchy and Resistance in the West Bank* (Boulder, CO: Lynne Rienner Publishers, 2001).

[18] For example, Beth Baron, *Egypt as a Woman: Nationalism, Gender, and Politics,* 1st paperback ed. (Berkeley, CA: University of California Press, 2007) and Margot Badran, *Feminists, Islam, and Nation: Gender and the Making of Modern Egypt* (Princeton, NJ: Princeton University Press, 1995).

[19] Heather J. Sharkey, *American Evangelicals in Egypt: Missionary Encounters in an Age of Empire* (Princeton: Princeton University Press, 2008).

[20] Catherine Mayeur-Jaouen, "Religieuses, laïques et travail social en Haute-Égypte: L'émergence de la question féminine à l'âge nationaliste (années 1940-1970)," *Social Sciences and Missions* 34:1-2 (2021), 29-61.

[21] This narrative and the following one are taken from Anne Zaki's collection from the series: #احكي_لي_يا_كنيسة .

sons and three daughters. Her father was a deacon in the Second Evangelical Church in Assiut. After obtaining a BA in Assiut she left for Cairo to enrol in the literature department at the University of Cairo. She then returned to Assiut after completing her studies to serve as a faculty member in the girls' academy which offered an educational system to help girls from Upper Egypt study and obtain a BA.

Given her distinguished character, when the American missions in Egypt left, their leaders selected Mathilde to further her educational journey in Assiut, thus fulfilling their vision of training girls from Upper Egypt. Mathilde married architect Louis Eklados, a widower of five sons. She helped him raise his children and they had a sixth son. Matilde was a busy mother in addition to her other major responsibilities. She was very active in her church. Mathilde served faithfully through the women's meetings in Assiut, as well as other surrounding churches. She had a significant role as a leader within the women's groups until her death at the age of 96 in 2018.

Mathilde is an example of how Arab women served in the mission field by pioneering educational opportunities for other girls and women. The second example I would like to look at is that of Awatef Wassef.

Awatef (Afifa) Fam Wassef: A Life of Worship and Dedication

Afifa was one of the first female students who attended the ETSC in the 1950s. Following her graduation, she left Fayyum and went to Luxor to serve as an evangelist where tradition forbade male preachers to address women. Her father, Fam Wassef, an elder in the Evangelical church in Sonores, had encouraged her. Her brother, Wasfy Fam, also an elder in the Evangelical church in Hilwan, encouraged her to take on this ministry despite being just in her twenties.

At that time, she also worked as a religion teacher in the American School in Luxor which later became known as Ramses College for Girls. In the 1960s, because of the presidential decision to Egyptianize schools, Afifa left Luxor and went back to Cairo to administer the first house for Christian students belonging to Azbakeya Evangelical Church. She served among female students for ten years until her marriage in 1970. Following her husband's four-year struggle with illness and eventual passing, she found herself alone, tasked with raising two children. Nevertheless, she continued to serve through the Sunday School Movement for fifteen years. Although weak eyesight made it difficult for her to read, she was committed to studying the scriptures until her death in 2021.

Reflection on the Role of Egyptian Women in Theological Education and Mission

Such women thrived in a creative milieu which helped them develop their thought and ministry. In a sense, they were pioneers in the changing discourse on mission and examples of the difficulties APW faced. Involvement in Sunday School to children, a ministry often exercised by women, is generally viewed as less important than preaching or pastoral leadership. But since thousands of children attend Sunday School across various ecclesial denominations in the Middle East, Arab women have a tremendous opportunity to invest in young lives; the astute reader will be able to link this characteristic with nurturing as a mark of mission. In the Eastern tradition, the Sunday School Movement was an extraordinary transmission of Protestant practice to the Coptic Church, which increasingly made space for Coptic women to be involved in mission. However, this discussion is beyond the scope of this chapter.[22]

In his monograph, Tharwat Adly discusses Egyptian Pentecostalism in the 20th century and its developments. Among other names, he makes mention of Western women such as Lilian Trasher (1887-1961).[23] Trasher was a young Pentecostal missionary to Egypt. Her legacy continued in the thriving ministry of the Lillian Trasher Orphanage, currently home to hundreds of orphans.

Etymology provides us with a simple but broad definition: missionaries are "sent" and see their action as rooted in a religious and civilization project–a phenomenon that can be viewed through several lenses including an institutional approach, ecclesiastical institutions, the effect of mission schools on local populations, gender studies, history of education, and transnational history.[24] One cannot deny that missionary efforts brought about transformation in the lives of women.

Amidst the acclaim for Western Protestant missions in the Middle East, counter-narratives exist. For example, the notion that Western missions claimed to be "the deliverer of women," and "the emblem of the 'modern' way of life" does not sit well with Palestinian Jean Said Makdisi.[25] According to Makdisi, the impact of Western missions was a sort of "marginalization," not elevation. She states: "In any case, the liberation of women, at least as we understand it today, was certainly not the aim of the missionaries: over and over again in their writings, they express the wish to make women better wives and mothers, not free women, a phrase which no doubt would have shocked them profoundly."[26] At the same time, the Western missionaries ignored "the appalling conditions of the masses of poor women in London and other urban centres, not to mention the peasants."[27]

However, the narrative that Arab women eagerly longed for salvation from the "degrading" cultural traditions is not to be disregarded, giving even greater purpose for the mission work. The missionaries contributed to transforming the lives of women. On their arrival, both Catholics and Protestants critically considered the situation of women in the Middle East. They viewed them as

---

[22] For more, see Habib Girgis, *The Fundamental Law for Coptic Orthodox Sunday Schools and the Coptic Youth Leagues in the See of St. Mark* (Cairo: The Central Committee for Coptic Orthodox Sunday Schools and the Coptic Youth League in the See of St. Mark, 1949, in Arabic).

[23] Tharwat Maher Nagib Adly Nagib, *Egyptian Pentecostalism: When Cyclones of Divine Power Invaded the Ancient Land: A Historiographical Analysis of Holiness, Pentecostal, and Neo-Charismatic Movements in Egypt in the Twentieth Century and Its Current Developments* (Leiden; Boston: Brill, 2023).

[24] Verdeil, "Mission Movements to and from the Middle East," 99-109 citing 99.

[25] Jean Said Makdisi, *Teta, Mother, and Me: Three Generations of Arab Women* (London: Saqi, 2005), 195-198.

[26] Makdisi, *Teta, Mother, and Me*, 193.

[27] Ibid., 191.

"poorly educated and married young…women aged quickly through the life of punishing labor."[28] In this regard, Chantal Verdeil elaborates: "It is clear that the education received, and the model imparted by the women missionaries (some of whom might have been the head of considerable organizations), gave Middle Eastern Women more resources to decide their own destinies."[29]

The second context I would like to consider is the Syrian and Lebanese context with special focus on Arab Biblewomen.

Arab Biblewomen/*Mubashirāt* in Syria and Lebanon

As a preamble to the 20th century period, in her thorough tracing of the history of missions in Syria (1860–1915), Deanna Womack demonstrates that "Syrian Protestant women and men emerged together as the primary agents – numerically and in terms of impact – in the encounter between missionaries and the broader Syrian society."[30] Although written accounts by Western missionaries of the day generally downplayed the role of APW, they in fact found their own space and made their voices and literary contributions heard. Instead of adhering to the general practice of allowing missionary men to speak "about them" and missionary women to speak "for them," Arab women made use of their own talents.[31] The first school for girls was established in Beirut in 1860.

Arab Biblewomen helped foreign women missionaries in their work in evangelism and social work as teachers, interpreters, Bible readers, and evangelists.[32] They were paid female evangelists who "tended to be less educated and socially marginalized …" and so they were rarely named within missionary reports.[33] It is said of the Syrian Biblewomen that they did not "directly confront patriarchy or demand equality."[34] Because individual Bible reading within Protestant missions was considered a priority, missionaries motivated women to interact with the scriptures personally. As a result, some missions in the 19th century employed Biblewomen to evangelize and pray with women and children. In turn, this revived the spiritual disciplines of the deaconesses of the earlier centuries.[35] The stories of Syrian women evangelists show that they had developed their "own spiritual authority in the Protestant community traditional clerical structures" despite their marginal status.[36]

The activities of *mubashirāt* (Biblewomen–in Arabic, literally women who share the good news) serve to provide a more coherent understanding of the roles of Syrian women in the missionary history of Syria beyond the circle of women

---

[28] Verdeil, "Mission Movements to and from the Middle East," 99-109 citing 100.
[29] Ibid., 99-109 citing 108.
[30] Womack, *Protestants, Gender and the Arab Renaissance in Late Ottoman Syria* (Edinburgh: Edinburgh University Press, 2019), 47.
[31] Ibid., 11.
[32] Ruth Tucker and Walter L. Liefeld, *Daughters of the Church: Women and Ministry from New Testament Times to the Present* (Grand Rapids: Academie Books, 1987), 340.
[33] Womack, *Protestants*, 155–156.
[34] Ibid., 296.
[35] Lindner, "Women," 405.
[36] Womack, *Protestants*, 11–12.

authors discussed in the previous section. Most *mubashirāt* did not leave written records of their activities and because the American Syria Mission did not include them in their writings it is difficult to unearth their work.[37] In the early 1890s, the British Syrian Mission (BSM) employed 24 women in its Bible mission. Between 1860 and 1915, there were more than 80 Arab *mubashirāt* diligently interpreting the scriptures, despite the fact that there "was no cultural precedent for women preachers in Syria."[38] The *nahdawī* women, who took part in the Arab cultural renaissance or *nahda*, were the first to write and publish. The influence of women's education later continued through the ongoing efforts of western mission organizations.

In 1924, the first women's college in Lebanon opened its doors in Beirut. It was administered by American Presbyterian missionaries. In the 1920s and 1930s, the American Junior College for Women was set up as a Christian institution with the purpose of establishing Christian principles of character in its students, which was a defining characteristic of all mission schools. As their purpose was to encourage women spiritually, the education had to include Christian studies. From the missionaries' perspective, women were the ideal receivers of Christian teachings.[39]

Further, many women influenced their society as ordained ministers and missionaries. Adèle Hajjar was the first Protestant woman to be ordained to ministry in Lebanon in 1920.[40] Hajjar was called to serve in Egypt and was described as "… the only fully qualified woman preacher we have in Syria, Palestine and Egypt … [She has] the language … the training … the experience … [and is] deeply spiritual," contrary to ordinary women in Egypt who were described as "famished" and "perishing."[41] Hajjar's passport reveals that she made at least one trip to either Alexandria or Assiut where she led Bible studies[42] and one to Palestine to attend a "feminist conference" in 1945.[43]

For APW, the establishment of educational institutions in their countries during the nineteenth century led to remarkable change. Without the mission-supported establishments, APW would have not been given educational opportunities until perhaps much later.

The following section sheds light on the contexts, lives and realities of APW in recent times and allows me to describe the contribution of APW in the present.

---

[37] Ibid., 277.

[38] Ibid., 277.

[39] Catherine Wadad Batruni, "Producing Pioneers: the American Junior College for Women and the Beirut College for Women, 1924-1973" (Doctor of Philosophy, American University of Beirut, 2019), 59. Retrieved from http://www.levantineheritage.com/pdf/Producing_Pioneers_The_American_Junior_College.pdf.

[40] Rima Nasrallah van Saane, "Adèle Jureidini Hajjar (1893-1971): The First Ordained Female Minister in Lebanon," *Theological Review* 27:2 (2006), 76–90.

[41] Ibid., 85–86.

[42] Ibid.

[43] Ibid., 84.

The Involvement of Women in Mission in Recent Decades

Middle Eastern Christianity has embodied a plurality of expressions across time and space. However, Middle Eastern Christian population is rapidly declining today.[44] Primarily as a consequence of emigration, Middle Eastern Christianity has expanded outside of its traditional heartland; there are now an estimated 7.7 million Middle Eastern Christians living outside the region. There have been two main migration waves–the first from the 1860s to the 1920s mainly from present-day Syria and Lebanon to North and Latin America, and the second from the 1950s onward.[45]

As a theological educator, I am privileged to interact with many female students who are involved in mission work in the Middle East and beyond.[46] Yet there are challenges that they encounter as they persist faithfully in following God's calling. Some of the challenges come from the difficult spiritual soil in the Middle East. Becoming a follower of Christ may entail being forsaken by family and friends, living a life where one carries the cross every day. Their hope is that it is a cross that is followed by resurrection. These are also women who are involved in theological education in different historical, cultural, and ecclesial contexts. Because there is uncertainty about the future of the church in the Middle East, complexity will remain as many Middle Eastern Christians join the diaspora. However, by their presence and engagement with the church and academy, APW are invited to reclaim their space in theological education. In so doing, they are called to be protective of their own roles as active agents and custodians of theological education. Though experiencing marginality, APW within theological education are resourceful and can shift their marginality to a position of influence and strength.

The fact that some women do not have the liberty to travel abroad to be involved in mission due to cultural limitations is a factor to consider as we reflect on the contribution of APW in the missionary context. Single women tend to express that their parents would only allow them to travel if they are chaperoned by a male figure. Some fathers may even discourage their daughters from engaging in theological education when it requires that they travel overseas. This account is in contrast to the several accounts of single Western female missionaries and researchers who have made their home in the Middle East.[47]

Inger-Marie Okkenhaug posits that "the history of women, gender and missions in the Middle East is a history of the intricate process of negotiating a personal vocation within the boundaries of expectations from the mission

---

[44] Deanna Womack, "Middle Eastern Christianity in the Context of World Christianity," in *Handbook of Christianity in the Middle East*, 548-558 citing 548.

[45] Fiona McCallum Guiney, "Middle Eastern Christianity outside the Middle East," in *Rowman & Littlefield Handbook of Christianity in the Middle East*, 559-571 citing 559.

[46] The lack of scholarship on Middle Eastern Christian women and on women's encounters with missionaries in the Middle East is documented in Akram Fouad Khater, *Embracing the Divine: Passion and Politics in the Christian Middle East* (Syracuse, NY: Syracuse University Press, 2011), 4–8.

[47] Inger Marie Okkenhaug, "Scandinavian Missionaries, Gender and Armenian Refugees during World War I: Crisis and Reshaping of Vocation," *Social Sciences and Missions* 23:1 (2010), 92.

establishment back home and the realities on the ground."[48] Historically, in all churches, formal theological education has been linked to the ordained ministry. However, in the 20th century lay theologians have emerged in some Western traditions.[49] Protestant Christianity could play a pioneering role in theological discourse in the Middle East by also engaging in some of these issues, particularly in relation to women.

APW are not just products of Western missions. Their authentic identity is a synthesis of Protestantism and Eastern Christianity, the latter being the original identity in which they have been rooted for more than two thousand years, and which combines the wider spectrum of their theological culture and history. This is true also for me as one originally from the Melkite Eastern tradition. Contemporary scholar Christopher D.L. Johnson argues that Eastern Christianity can be "resuscitated" by Western influence.[50] Western Protestant missionaries self-consciously understand themselves as having the ability to reform Eastern Christianity in the context of reformist theological and ecclesial culture. However, Johnson understates, as did many missionaries, the distinctive ecclesial character of Christianity in the Middle East which is marked by deep historical complexity and plurality. Therefore, the need for an ecumenical theological endeavour is essential in the Middle East, particularly for women.

The authoritative voice that APW have enables them to articulate their present way of doing missions through the creative exercise of their own study, research, and writing. In this way, APW bring their own creativity to their theological exercise by drawing on their unique assets not found in Western Christian women. For example, their fluency in Arabic, in addition to the Eastern Christian languages such as Assyrian, Armenian, Coptic, and their diverse experiences as a result of persecution, set them apart from Western Christian women. In the context of the Middle East, there is indeed persecution and a lack of freedom for Christians, but these women have a profound and rich voice which needs to be heeded.

In the last decades women within the Protestant tradition, such as the following have contributed to missions through theological education, their writings and their ecclesial contributions: Mary Mikhael, Najla Kassab, Rima Nasrallah, Mathilde Sabbagh, Anne Zaki and Roula Mansour. Their growing (influential, significant, important, powerful) voices are an irreplaceable influence for the coming generation as we look to the next ten years in the Middle

---

[48] Inger-Marie Okkenhaug, "Introduction: Gender and Missions in the Middle East," *Social Sciences and Missions* 23:1 (2010), 1-6 citing 3.

[49] For example, Stefanie Hugh-Donovan's research work concerned the leading lay theologian Oliver Clément (1921-2009). For his wider ecumenical and ecclesiological context see Hugh-Donavan's studies, for example, Stefanie Hugh-Donovan, "Olivier Clément on Orthodox Theological Thought and Ecclesiology in the West," *International Journal for the Study of the Christian Church* 10:2–3 (May 2010), 116–129, https://doi.org/10.1080/1474225X.2010.492270.

[50] Christopher D. L. Johnson, "'He Has Made the Dry Bones Live': Orientalism's Attempted Resuscitation of Eastern Christianity," *Journal of the American Academy of Religion* 82:3 (September 2014), 811–840, https://doi.org/10.1093/jaarel/lfu036.

East. Theologian Eleni Kasselouri reminds us that "[t]he early church developed its ecclesiology, and in turn its missionary practice, on a radical eschatological teaching of the historical Jesus about the kingdom of God which…moves dialectically between the 'already' and the 'not yet'; in other words, it has begun already in the present but will be completed in its final authentic form in the eschaton."[51] As APW are situated in the "not yet," they eagerly participate in the expansion of God's kingdom. And contexts, like people, are always dynamic and changing. The gospel is moving forward. One cannot exclude more than fifty percent of the congregation from contributing, particularly in a highly challenging context where it is essential to draw on every person's resources. As I observed recently, while only Protestant churches have ordained female priests – in Lebanon, Syria, and the Palestinian territories – other courageous figures are paving an emerging path of spirituality within the parameters of patriarchal Arab society.[52]

While remaining deeply rooted in their own local culture, women have a missionary role within their own church with a message that women ought to have a voice. The default missiology seems to focus on the role of men.[53] Arab Protestant Women's perspectives and ability to think strategically in mission work would enrich the understanding and practices of theological education whereas often they have not been invited to assume other visible leadership roles. However, Arab Protestant women are transitioning from the mission-historical context. As I seek to describe Christianity in the context of the world, not only as the Christianity of the 19th century, but also as the Christianity of the 21st century, I have found that describing "the other" is helpful. As a Protestant Christian, finding ways to collaborate with other Christian traditions is important. I am indebted to the witness of Eastern Christianity in the form of the contribution of its many Eastern women, and the way that their faith and contributions can enrich and inform our participation in the church and theological education as Protestant women. Retrieving the reality of Eastern Christianity can challenge mainstream mission-established Protestantism. By making this serious historical point, we are at a moment of significant contribution as most Arab Protestant women have an Eastern Christian background. Arab Protestants have something to offer to the broader church and women can and should be part of who offers it.

Many Arab Protestant women have shown positive appreciation of the role of Western female missionaries. This appreciation provides further insights on which I as a researcher can build. Although the context of Western female

---

[51] Eleni Kasselouri-Hatzivassiliadi, "Mission, Gender, and Theological Education: An Orthodox Perspective," *International Review of Mission* 104:1 (2015), 38.

[52] Grace Al-Zoughbi, "Today's Arab Women Theologians Have Plenty of Past Exemplars," *Christianity Today*, 30 June 2023, https://www.christianitytoday.com/ct/2023/june-web-only/women-theologians-middle-east-desert-mothers-hindiyya-irini.html.

[53] Pam Arlund and Regina Foard, "From Her Perspective: Women and Multiplication Movement," in *Motus Dei: The Movement of God to Disciple the Nations,* ed. Warrick Farah, Dave Coles, James Lucas, and Jonathan Andrews (Littleton, CO: William Carey Library, 2021), 176–198, citing 176.

missionaries is different to the Arab contexts, they have been pivotal in encouraging Arab Protestant women. However, the role models they provide are still essentially Western, which accentuates the need for local Arab role models. Looking for an insider model does not negate the influence of the outsider model, particularly those who desire to become insiders such as the Western missionaries. The significant contributions of Western female missionaries deserve further dedicated study.

Conclusion

Mission is an essential expression of our faith. As an Arab Christian woman, my life has been transformed through fulfilling God's calling. Conducting research on women in the Middle East has changed me. I am much more aware of how their story shapes who I am as a Protestant woman from an Eastern Christian heritage. The contribution of Arab women to missions is an ongoing conversation. What we are witnessing is Arab Protestant women participating in missions not only to their own community, but also to global Christianity.

I commenced this article by drawing attention to the narrative of the Samaritan woman. Although marginalized and from a different ethno-religious community, this woman engaged in a remarkable theological discourse with Jesus. Her first need was not for water, it was for repentance. Jesus gave her both. The example Jesus offers to us through his conversation with the Samaritan woman recorded in John 4 reminds us that no one should be on the margins, not even a Samaritan woman with a difficult history. Jesus invites her into a relationship with Him, into the kingdom, and thus into gaining theological understanding. Theological education should uncompromisingly speak to the context. Where theological education is occurring, it needs to be in conversation with the churches about openness to women's participation in the various fields which comprise theology. Theological education must be contextualized, but it must also challenge, where necessary, the contexts in which it takes place. The narrative of the Samaritan woman reminds us that we are collaborators with Christ making way for the further participation of Arab women in mission. Despite many obstacles, despite incidents of imprisonment, and even martyrdom, the gospel went forward because of the commitment of Christ's male and female followers, empowered by the Spirit, obedient to his word. Highlighting the role of Arab women can envision and call into being the emergence of future roles for women, particularly a lay theological community of women mission scholars. Dialoguing with other women scholars in different traditions allows for a wider ecumenical exchange and discussion within this ecclesial plurality. This is only the beginning, but what a beginning.

Cooperation between Foreign Mission Agencies and Local Protestant Churches: The Case of the Christian Endeavor Union and the Armenian Evangelical Churches[1]

Asadour Manjrian

Introduction

The Protestant churches of the Middle East, which were established in the 19th century, owe a historical debt to missionary agencies from Europe and North America. In the 20th century, the ecumenical century, the shape of their relationship changed. This chapter traces the relation between the Christian Endeavor movement and the Armenian Evangelical Churches of Syria and Lebanon. The special interest of this case is that the Christian Endeavor was not a typical missionary society, but had the fostering of church life among the youth as its specific interest.

The Christian Endeavor (CE) was first established in Portland, Maine, in 1881. It was initially called the Young People's Society of Christian Endeavor. It was a nondenominational movement that focused on organizing religious meetings for young people. Just like many other Protestant missionary agencies, it emerged in a revivalist, mission-focused Protestant context. The purpose of the CE was to stimulate personal spirituality and missionary engagement among young people in Protestant churches. It was especially effective in congregational churches.

In the Middle East, the CE has worked primarily though not exclusively with the Armenian Evangelical churches. These churches emerged from a revival movement within the Armenian Apostolic (Orthodox) Church and were formed into a denomination in 1846, when they were recognised as a "millet" (an independent religious legal entity with its own laws and regulations), by the Ottoman authorities in Constantinople. From the outset, the Armenian Evangelicals were under indigenous leadership, and self-governance was never a problem. The Armenian Evangelicals also highly valued lay involvement and adopted a congregational policy.[2]

The cooperation between the Christian Endeavor and the Armenian Evangelical churches dates to early 20th century, but the focus of this chapter is

---

[1] This chapter is an adaptation of a thesis that was submitted by the author to the Near East School of Theology in Beirut as part of the requirements for its Master of Divinity programme. The thesis work was supervised by Wilbert van Saane, who has also helped adapt the thesis to the purposes of this volume. The research, the analysis, and the presentation of the material are the work of the author.

[2] Hovhannes Aharonian. *The Armenian Evangelical Church on the Crossroads* (Beirut: Union of the Armenian Evangelical Churches in Near East, 1988) 61-62.

on the period after World War I and the Armenian Genocide (1915). Since the 1920s, many Armenian Evangelicals in the Middle East have been active members of a CE group. It is reasonable to suppose that the CE has shaped their spirituality and missionary involvement. The aim of this chapter is to trace the work of the CE among Middle Eastern Christians, especially Armenian Evangelicals, and to map their areas of cooperation.

This chapter describes the origins of the CE movement and its dissemination in Syria and Lebanon. It then moves on to trace and analyze the mission of the CE groups and their relation to the Armenian Evangelical churches. Its mission in Syria and Lebanon is characterized as "inner mission" and its relation to the churches as symbiotic. Using Geoffrey Wainwright's adaptation of the famous typology of Richard Niebuhr to spirituality, its attitude towards the societies of Syria and Lebanon in general and the Armenian subcultures within it in particular is described as paradoxical.

Origin of the Christian Endeavor Movement

In the late 19th century, a number of new Anglo-Saxon Protestant agencies emerged that were focused on young people. On the one hand, church leaders felt that there was a need to foster such movements for young people; on the other, a missionary initiative and desire lay with young people themselves. Out of these concerns emerged organizations such as the Young Men's Christian Association (YMCA), the Young Women's Christian Association (YWCA), the Student Christian Movement (SCM), and the World Student Christian Federation (WSCF).[3] These lay movements would play an important role in the history of the ecumenical movement and the World Council of Churches (WCC), as they were non-denominational and easily facilitated ecumenical connections between members of different churches. They had an evangelical basis, and their aims were evangelization and mission. At the same time, these movements stimulated their members to actively participate in their local congregations and denominations.

The founder of the Christian Endeavor Union was Francis Clark (1851-1927). It was his desire to spiritually energise Protestant youth and to lead them to service. As pastor of Williston Congregational Church in Portland, Maine, he started inviting some of the young members of his community to his house.[4] During one of these meetings, on 2 February 1881, something new happened. Clark asked the 40-50 members who were present to sign a pledge.[5] After the young people signed the pledge the first Society of the Christian Endeavor was established.

---

[3] Ruth Rouse & Stephen Charles Neill, *A History of The Ecumenical Movement 1517-1948* (London: SPCK, 1967), 599.

[4] Francis Clark, *Christian Endeavor in All Lands* (Boston: United Society of Christian Endeavor, 1906), 35.

[5] Francis Clark, *The Christian Endeavor Manual* (Boston and Chicago: United Society of Christian Endeavor, 1925), 11, 13-14.

In his writings, Clark revealed his initial concerns about the success of the pledge that he had written and given the young members to sign.[6] These fears were understandable in light of the previous unsuccessful attempts to create a youth movement within this church. But Clark persevered, motivated by the phrase "faith triumphant over our fear."[7] Two days after this meeting, a prayer meeting took place. It was different from previous prayer meetings. The 40 attendees recited verses from scripture, gave testimonies of their faith, and sang hymns together. It was the first prayer meeting in the history of the Christian Endeavor movement.[8]

In the pledge there were six covenantal or solemn promises. Some of these concerned the member's personal faith and participation in the local church, while others concerned their membership of the Christian Endeavor: daily reading of the Bible, daily prayer, support of the local church, attendance of midweek meetings of the society, active participation in it, and, in case of absence, the sending of a Bible verse to be read aloud at the meeting.[9]

The motto of the Christian Endeavor Union articulated by Francis Clark was "for Christ and the Church."[10] These two elements were not to be understood as separated from each other. The idea was that members of the CE would serve Christ by serving their churches. In addition to this watchword, there were four fundamental concepts which defined the identity of the Christian Endeavor Union and which revealed its missionary, ecclesiastical, and ecumenical nature:

- Confession of Christ: accepting Christ as personal saviour and professing this;
- Service for Christ, understood as service to the church and to people outside the church;
- Loyalty to Christ's church; as was made explicit in the pledge, the CE expected its members to be committed to their local church communities;
- Fellowship with all Christ's people; preservation of the faith in Christ through the community of believers.[11]

These principles show that the main objective of the CE was to serve local Protestant congregations, while maintaining an ecumenical openness. One of the ways in which this objective was pursued was by preparing young leaders. The CE has maintained an emphasis on leadership training throughout its history. This emphasis on leadership was based on the premise that every church is in constant need of lay leaders for ministries such as Sunday school. The method of raising and training leaders was to ask members to attend classes, and to transition from one level to another. Members who had gone through all the levels qualified for the graduation, which took place on the first Sunday of every

---

[6] Clark, *Christian Endeavor in All Lands*, 36.

[7] Ibid., 43.

[8] Ibid., 44.

[9] Clark, *The Christian Endeavor Manual*, 58.

[10] Bert Davis, *Leadership through Christian Endeavor* (Boston and Chicago: International Society of Christian Endeavor, 1931), 19.

[11] Davis, *Leadership through Christian Endeavor*, 19-23; Clark, *The Christian Endeavor Manual*, 21.

February, commemorating the start of the movement. It was called "Promotion Day."[12]

The growth of the society was gradual and can be mainly attributed to Francis Clark and his travels around the world. Clark became the President of the Society, and in the forty years of his presidency, made nineteen international voyages to expand the organization.[13] In 1884, the Christian Endeavor was established in China.[14] In 1887 there were some societies in England, and in 1888 the first society in Australia was established.[15] As the next section demonstrates, Christian Endeavor branches were also started in the Middle East. Today there are national societies in 30 different countries around the world: seven in North America, nine in Europe, six in Asia, nine in Australia and the Pacific, and some scattered in Africa.[16]

The Christian Endeavor Union in Syria and Lebanon

The presence of large Armenian communities in Syria and Lebanon goes back to the First World War and especially to 1915, when the Ottoman authorities organized a series of massacres of non-Turks who were living under Ottoman rule. The highest number of victims were among the Armenians. According to many reports, the number of Armenian people who died reached 1.5 million and around 500,000 people were displaced from their lands, which were located in what is today the southern and eastern part of Turkey. Many were deported to Syria by a decision of the Minister of Interior Talaat Pasha, and many moved to Lebanon, where they lived as refugees.[17]

Some reports show that CE societies already existed among Armenians in Ottoman lands. In his two books *Memoirs of Many Men in Many Lands* and *Christian Endeavor in All Lands*, Clark wrote about the countries he visited and about the people he encountered. He reports that, in 1893, he visited the Ottoman Empire and met a missionary called James Fowle.[18] Fowle began his work as a preacher in Caesarea in 1878. When Fowle returned to Caesarea in 1890, after visiting the United States, he found a pastor in Yozgat who was leading a group of young men and boys. This was a Christian Endeavor Society, and they were doing the same work as the Christian Endeavor societies in the United States.[19]

---

[12] Davis, *Leadership Through Christian Endeavor*, 27-31.
[13] Jason Lanker, "Francis E. Clark: Founder of Christian Endeavor," *Christian Education Journal: Research on Educational Ministry* 11:2 (2014), 383-391, https://doi.org/10.1177/073989131401100211.
[14] Clark, *Christian Endeavor in All Lands*, 68.
[15] Clark, *The Christian Endeavor Manual*, 17.
[16] Christian Endeavor, "About Christian Endeavor," accessed 20 November 2020, http://worldsceunion.org/about_us.
[17] Ninan Koshy, *Armenia: The Continuing Tragedy* (Geneva: Commission of the Churches on International Affairs & World Council of Churches, 1984), 12-13.
[18] Francis Clark, *Memories of Many Men in Many Lands* (Boston and Chicago: United Society of Christian Endeavor, 1922) 120.
[19] James Fowle, "Out-Stations of Cesarea," *Missionary Herald* 86:5 (1890), 194.

It is unclear whether this society was the result of the work of Fowle or other influences.

Clark and his wife Harriet faced difficulties in shipping books because of the Ottoman restrictions. Clark reports that his wife tried to smuggle Bibles and other Christian writings, which were confiscated by the Turkish officials. In Mersin, Clark met an Armenian pastor and in Istanbul he found an Armenian Evangelical Church in which a Christian Endeavor Society was active. Clark was invited to speak at that church, and he writes that during his speech he felt uncomfortable. Later he learned that a Turkish spy soldier was present in the meeting and that the words "union," "fellowship," "brotherhood," "Christian Endeavor," and other words were not supposed to be mentioned in the church because of their political connotations.[20] Clark mentioned that, although societies such as the Christian Endeavor were prohibited by law, there were at least eight functioning societies in Harpoot, Mardin, Marash, Caesarea, Smyrna, Constantinople, Erzerum, Van,[21] and Adapazar (from 1906 to 1914).[22]

Although officially one might say that the Christian Endeavor Union in Syria and Lebanon was launched in some churches starting from 1923, we can trace its presence in Aleppo at least 19 years earlier. In 1904, a Mrs Altounian from England had visited the city and explained to Armenian Christians how the Christian Endeavor Union played an important role among young people in Europe. She suggested creating something similar in Aleppo.[23] The result was regular prayer meetings for young women.

The first official CE Society in the Armenian Evangelical churches in the Near East was started in Aleppo, Syria in 1923, in the Armenian Evangelical Emmanuel Church by Hovhanness Shnorhokian and Najib Shirikjian.[24] The first worship service of this CE society took place on Sunday, November 24, 1923.[25] Later in the same year, the second society of Christian Endeavor was launched in Aleppo, in the Armenian Evangelical Bethel Church. In the following years, all the Armenian Evangelical churches in Syria and Lebanon that belonged to the Union of Armenian Evangelical churches in the Near East, had their own CE societies and gradually these became part of the church's established youth ministry. The political conditions in Syria under the French Mandate were different from those in Ottoman Turkey and Christian associations could be freely established and registered.

We can conclude that the Christian Endeavor societies were first introduced in the Armenian Evangelical churches of the Ottoman Empire. The societies

---

20 Clark, *Memories of Many Men*, 120-129.

21 Clark, *Christian Endeavor in All Lands*, 435.

22 Piouzant Apigian, "A Christian Youth Society in Adapazar from 1904 to 1914," *CHANASSER* 18:4 (1955), 127.

23 Arousiag Markarian Sinanian, "When Did the Christian Endeavor Union in Aleppo Start?" *CHANASSER* 20:2 (1957), 50. Markarian Sinanian writes that she was one of the members of that group that started prayer meetings for young women.

24 Dikran Khrlopian, *The Golden Book, Vol. 1* (Beirut: Union of Armenian Evangelical Churches in Near East, 1950), 145.

25 (No Author), "Youth in Movement," *CHANASSER* 6:3 (1943), 63.

were founded upon impulses from North America and Europe, including visits by missionaries and travelling Armenians, but they were, from the beginning, led by members of local Armenian Evangelical congregations and were rather informal in nature. After the Genocide, these societies were restarted by Armenians diaspora in Syria and Lebanon, this time in a more official capacity.

The overlap in membership of the Christian Endeavor societies and the Armenian churches was indeed such that soon the societies felt the need to be in close partnership with the Union of Armenian Evangelical Churches in the Near East. The first General Assembly of the combined societies (the Union) took place in Aleppo in 1930, with representatives of the Syrian and Lebanese societies in attendance.[26]

The Christian Endeavor Union in Syria and Lebanon had two types of societies. The first one was for young people who were above 17 years of age and the second was for teenagers in the age group 13-16.[27] Active members of the youth society promised to "strive to know God, to have a consistent relationship with God by praying, reading the Scripture, and through spiritual worship services."[28] They also promised to be committed and work for the prosperity of the church's spiritual, ethical, and financial aspects. Beyond the church, active members had duties concerning the Armenian community. Active members were expected to promote the spiritual, ethical, and cultural principles of the CE Union in society.

The local manifestations of the Christian Endeavor remained embedded in the international movement. The Christian Endeavor Union in Syria and Lebanon was closely connected to the World Christian Endeavor mission. It remained an active member of the World Christian Endeavor Union. Members from Syria and Lebanon participated in the World Christian Endeavor conventions, which took place every four years. Recently, Rev. Raffi Messerlian, pastor of an Armenian Evangelical Church in Beirut and an active leader in the Christian Endeavor Union in Syria and Lebanon, was elected president of the World Christian Endeavor Union in 2019 and 2023.

Having outlined the early history of the Christian Endeavor movement in Lebanon and Syria, we are now in a position to consider some of its expressions of mission in the region and to consider its cooperation with the local churches.

For Christ: The Mission of the Christian Endeavor Union in the Near East

Many (if not all) who contributed to establishment of the societies and became members were survivors of the Armenian Genocide. While the groups in Syria and Lebanon followed the general pattern of CE groups, they also rendered a unique service to these survivors. Their mission was to gather these young people, who had been children or infants at the time of the genocide. Many of

---

[26] Khrlopian, *The Golden Book*, 148-149.

[27] Union of Armenian Evangelical Churches in the Near East and Christian Endeavor Union, *Bylaws* (Beirut: Christian Endeavor Union, Beirut, 1992), 5.

[28] Ibid., 2.

them were orphans. The CE movement gave them a new sense of belonging and the hope that what had been lost in the homeland of the Armenians could be re-established.

Missionary Activity during the French Mandate Period

The mission of the Christian Endeavor groups also stretched beyond the Armenian communities, especially during the interbellum. On many occasions the societies went outside their churches and organized worship services with and for others. In the 1930s, the group at the Armenian Evangelical Church of Emmanuel in Aleppo went on mission trips to the villages outside that city and organized worship services for teenagers. In the countryside, they conducted worship services in a hospital and they also organized social gatherings for soldiers from Madagascar, who were serving in Syria during the French Mandate.[29] In 1939, the Damascus group organized a debate on the book *Islam and Christianity Face to Face*.[30] These examples show that, in their early years, the type of missionary work in which the CE societies engaged took them outside their Armenian community and, in light of the traumatic experiences during the Genocide, outside their comfort zone. At this stage, the mission of the CE could be characterized as spiritual service and seeking dialogue.

After the end of the French mandate in Syria and Lebanon no such missionary activities were reported in the publications of the CE Union. The French mandate permitted the Christian missionary organizations to function and move freely and easily. After the French troops left the Middle East and Syria and Lebanon gained their independence, missionary work began to be associated with colonialism and was restricted, especially by the Syrian government. This may be a reason for the cessation of this type of missionary activity by the CE movement.

Missionary Activity in Independent Syria and Lebanon

As the Christian Endeavor Union became more organized and institutionalized within the Armenian Evangelical churches its mission slowly changed to an "inner mission." The term "inner mission" was often used in relation to the Social Gospel movement at the beginning of the 20th century. Richard Pierard distinguishes three aspects or types of "inner mission": first, fighting systems that, by their very nature, are harmful to society and individuals; second, seeking to increase a sense of morality and spirituality on the levels of the individual and the church; and third, spreading the kingdom of God through piety and morality.[31] It appears that the CE groups of Syria and Lebanon worked on all

---

[29] Y. Tovmassian, "Discoveries From Societies' Reports," *CHANASSER* 1:1 (1937), 12.

[30] (No Author), "Endeavor on the Move," *CHANASSER* 2:3 (1939), 82. The title that was discussed was Hohannes K. Krikorian, *Islam and Christianity Face to Face* (New York: Gotchnag Press, 1937).

[31] Richard V. Pierard, "Inner Mission," in *The Encyclopedia of Christianity, Volume 2*, ed. Erwin Fahlbusch et al., trans. Geoffrey Bromiley (Grand Rapids, MI/ Cambridge, UK: William B. Eerdmans Publishing Company and Leiden/ Boston/ Köln: Brill, 2001), 706-708.

three levels during the first few decades of their existence, but that work on the first level became more difficult after these countries had become independent.

Five types of activities characterized the mission of the Christian Endeavor Societies. First, they organized regular prayer meetings. This was a form of youth mission that was already present in the churches. Not all members had accepted Christ as their Lord and Saviour. The weekly meeting, especially the teenagers' meetings, were used as opportunities to teach and talk about Jesus with a view of a personal conversion and commitment.

Second, the CE groups reached out to the schools that belonged to the Union of Armenian Evangelical Churches in the Near East. The CE Union never established or managed schools, but its leaders often visited the church schools to introduce the Christian Endeavor and to invite the students to join the meetings. Schools that belonged to the Union of Armenian Evangelical Churches in the Near East had regular morning chapels, which took place a few times a week before classes. These usually included songs, a Bible reading, and a short message. Leaders of the local CE society were often invited to speak during these chapels. It was hoped that the students of the school who were not committed to faith in Christ would become members of the local CE society and grow in faith there. It is important to note that evangelism in the schools was not just the work of the CE leaders but also its members. It was common that students who attended the weekly prayer meeting invited their friends.

The third arena of mission was practical service, organized either by the local society or the CE Executive Committee. The CE groups addressed physical as well as spiritual needs, sometimes offering financial, humanitarian, psychological, and moral support.

The fourth expression of mission of the CE Union were the Daily Vacation Bible Schools (DVBS). These summer schools were conducted in close cooperation with the local churches, often taking place on the school grounds, over four to six weeks in the summer vacation. They were attended by students aged between 3 and 12 years. The programmes of the summer schools included worship services, Bible lessons, songs, games, Armenian cultural activities or talks, dance, music, art, and crafts. The summer schools were partially funded by the Christian Endeavor Executive Committee and the leaders of the summer schools were mostly members of the local CE societies.

The fifth and perhaps the most influential expression of mission were the summer camps. Every year, the CE in Syria and Lebanon organized camps for different age groups. The first age group was 6-11. From the 1950s until 1985, summer camps were organized for children who were disadvantaged and could not otherwise afford to go to camps. Another camp was for children who attended the Sunday Schools of the Armenian Evangelical churches. The second age group was 12 to 17 and the third age group was for those over 18. These camps were tailored for members of the local societies. The CE Executive members were responsible for appointing the leaders and developing the themes of the camps. The camps took place at rural camp/conference centres and their main aim was to create an atmosphere for growth in faith and devotion to God. The retreat setting, away from home and the worries of the world, was thought to be conducive to this. The camps often included an altar call or other invitation to commit oneself to faith in Christ.

As was mentioned, the CE's mission outside the churches remained rather limited, especially when we compare it to the work of other organizations such as Youth for Christ or the InterVarsity Fellowship. There are two reasons for this. First, there was a language barrier. The CE was managed by Armenians and, after the French Mandate ended, virtually all activities were conducted in Armenian. This hampered the CE's missionary outreach to Arabic speakers. Second, the CE's strong attachment to the church, which was always its first mandate and mission, may have hindered its flexibility in outreach beyond the church's walls. The embedding of the CE societies in the Armenian Evangelical Churches gave it a clear focus and a degree of institutionalization, but it carried the constant risk of serving them and the wider Armenian community alone. The following section considers the symbiosis of the CE societies and the churches more closely.

For the Church: The Relationship of the Christian Endeavor Movement with the Armenian Evangelical Churches in the Near East

A prominent Armenian Evangelical leader once said: "The CE is tomorrow's Church."[32] The close relationship between the CE Union and the Union of Armenian Evangelical Churches and the individual CE societies with their churches has also been compared to the relationship between parents and their children.[33] Before becoming a Union with a committee and before having offices and activities, the Christian Endeavor started in local churches, as has been mentioned earlier. First, congregation members established their local CE societies, then they decided to come together to form the Christian Endeavor Union in Syria and Lebanon. The CE Union itself cannot stand alone and this can be seen clearly from its bylaws, which state that its first loyalty lies with the Union of the Armenian Evangelical Churches.[34] It is also important to note that the CE follows the chief ecclesiological principles of the Armenian Evangelical Church.

The definition of "church" of the Union of Armenian Evangelical Churches in the Near East is that it is "the body of Christ and the community of believers."[35] Since the CE Union is the bond of local CE societies, which are located within the churches that are part of the Union of Armenian Evangelical Churches, the local CE societies also consider themselves part of the whole body of Christ and part of the community of believers. What then, one might ask, does this mean? How can a youth organization be part of the body of Christ and the community of believers? And what is the role of the CE societies and the Union

---

[32] Hovhannes Karjian, "CE Is Also a Church," *CHANASSER* 46:2 (1983), 26.

[33] Mardiros Marganian, *Christian Endeavor Union* (Beirut: Union of Sunday Schools in the Holy Bible Countries, 1935), 41.

[34] Union of Armenian Evangelical Churches in the Near East and Christian Endeavor Union, *Bylaws* (Beirut: Union of Armenian Evangelical Churches in Near East, 1974),1.

[35] Ibid. 35.

within the church? Here we need to consider the nature of the relation between church and parachurch, a much-debated matter among evangelicals.

Administrative Interweaving

It is worth noting that the relationship between the church and the CE society can be viewed from two perspectives. Regarding the church's involvement, the pastor of the local church is almost always the president of the local CE Society and the elders of the church generally appoint a main leader for the group, who should be a communicant member of the church.[36] Communicant membership is the official full membership of the churches of the Union of Armenian Evangelical Churches in the Near East. To become a communicant member, candidates must take classes about the church, its history, and their rights and responsibilities as communicant members. Having completed the classes, they give a testimony in front of the congregation to obtain the communicant membership of the church, which includes some commitments.

From the perspective of the teenagers, the involvement of the church is even more direct. All leaders of the teenage groups are jointly appointed by the CE youth (18+) committee and the council of elders.[37] In addition, the composition of the Executive Committee of the CE Union also reflects the close relationship between this organization and the churches. Historically, many pastors have been members of this committee. Moreover, according to the bylaws, at least seven out of twelve members of the Executive Committee of the CE Union should be communicant members in the Armenian Evangelical churches.[38]

Cross-Fertilization in Spirituality

When considering spirituality, what stands out is the CE's contribution to music, hymnody, and liturgy in the Armenian Evangelical churches. Over the years, the CE Union published different hymnals, the most significant of which was *Nor Yerk Yerketsek Deroch* (Sing a New Song to the Lord) by Rev. Nerses Balabanian in 1996.[39] This hymnal was gradually adopted by the congregations and continues to be an important source for worship in the Union of Armenian Evangelical Churches in the Near East. Today, it is not only used in the meetings of the youth and teenagers, but also during Sunday morning service in some of the local churches. In addition to the publications of song books, the CE organized choirs, which perform concerts in the local churches and sometimes to broader audiences.

The spirituality of the CE Union in the Middle East has not been stagnant. It has changed and developed over time, even if the basic characteristics have remained constant. Members are expected to submit their lives to Christ; to be faithful in personal prayers, scripture reading and meditation; to demonstrate moral integrity; and to faithfully attend the meetings. They are expected to lead

---

[36] Ibid., 3

[37] Ibid., 5.

[38] Ibid., 7.

[39] Nerses Balabanian. *Nor Yerk Yerketsek Deroch / Sing New Song to Lord* (Beirut: Christian Endeavor Union, 1996).

lives of personal devotion and moral uprightness. Camps and weekly prayer meetings are important occasions to teach the values of Christian living. The CE Union and its societies do not approve of "nominal Christianity," in which people are careless about their relationship with God.[40] The CE aims to lead its members to a life of holiness and growth in God's image by imitating Christ. The spirituality of the CE Union may therefore be appropriately called a pietistic, revivalist Protestant spirituality. As mentioned earlier, the Armenian Evangelical churches arose from a renewal movement within the Armenian Orthodox Church but were also influenced by the same revivalist spirituality of American missionaries in the 19th century. Many of these missionaries hailed from congregationalist milieus in North America. It is no wonder, then, that the CE movement found such a congenial spiritual environment in the Armenian Evangelical churches.

A Symbiotic and Paradoxical Relationship

The place of the CE societies within the Armenian Evangelical churches may be characterized as *ecclesiola in ecclesia*, a term from the Pietist movement meaning small churches within the church. This statement might be misleading. It should not be taken to mean that the CE took the place of the church or called itself a church. In reality, the CE movement could have not been possible without the support and contributions from the local churches to this youth movement.

Based on Richard Niebuhr's typology of Christianity in relation to culture, Geoffrey Wainwright has proposed five types of Christian spirituality in relation to culture.[41] According to Wainwright, Christian spirituality can be characterized, first, as "Christ against Culture." This is a spirituality that presupposes a fundamental conflict between the kingdom of God and the kingdom of the world. The second type of spirituality is that of the "Christ of Culture," meaning that the church and the state or the culture are closely related and difficult to separate. Historically, this model was embodied during the time of Emperor Constantine and the Byzantine period that followed. Third, "Christ above Culture" indicates that the culture is neither perfect nor evil, and that spiritually is about what transcends cultures. Fourth, "Christ and Culture in Paradox" is a model that stands between the first and the second model but leans towards the first, countercultural model. The paradox-model presupposes that human nature is not entirely evil, but nevertheless emphasizes that Christians

---

[40] For a consideration of the phrase "nominal Christianity" as used by Protestant missionaries to the Middle East, see Habib Badr, "Mission to Nominal Christians: The Policy and Practice of the American Board of Commissioners for Foreign Missions and Its Missionaries Concerning Easter Churches which Led to the Organization of a Protestant Church in Beirut (1819-1848)" (PhD diss., Princeton Theological Seminary, 1992).

[41] Alister McGrath, *Christian Spirituality: An Introduction* (Malden, MA, and Oxford, UK: Blackwell, 1999), 19. Richard Niebuhr's typology, proposed in his book *Christ and Culture* (Harper, New York, 1951), was applied to Christian Spirituality by Geoffrey Wainwright in his chapter on types of spirituality in C. Jones, G. Wainwright, and E. Yarnold, *The Study of Spirituality* (London: SPCK, 1986).

have to struggle to live authentic Christian lives. The fifth model, "Christ the Transformer of the Culture," has similarities with the third model, "Christ Above Culture." "Christ the Transformer of the Culture" characterizes a spirituality that is concerned with the present time and argues that the elevation of human nature took place through the incarnation.

While we can find some of the characteristics of every model in the spirituality of the CE Union of Syria and Lebanon, I think that the fourth type, "Christ and culture in paradox," describes its spirituality best. The reason for choosing this model is the relation of the CE Union's ambivalent relation to the Armenian identity as well as Syrian and Lebanese identity. The CE's spirituality as it is found in the Middle East is not purely countercultural. The CE does not isolate itself from the culture but challenges its members to be part of their society with their specific values. In its early decades, CE groups attempted to transform culture through service and dialogue. We have also observed that the CE societies fostered and celebrated Armenian cultural expressions. At the same time, the focus was always on personal spirituality and a lifestyle that included some characteristics that were not necessarily present in the culture. This implied the conflict between the kingdom of God and the kingdom of earth. Historically, a choice for the Christ and culture in paradox-model is logical, because of the roots of the CE Union in American revivalist evangelicalism, which in turn owed much to Pietism.

The relationship of the CE movement and the churches was, as mentioned before, not one-sided. The churches gave leadership and legitimacy to the CE and the CE contributed to the churches, especially by raising and training leaders and by preparing young people to become members. This preparation of young people to become members was a constant in the CE's history in the Middle East. To illustrate, in 1928, five years after its establishment, the CE of the Armenian Evangelical Bethel Church and the Armenian Evangelical Emmanuel Church (both in Aleppo) contributed 44 communicant members to their churches.[42] In the First Armenian Evangelical Church of Beirut, more than twenty CE members became communicant members in the years 1962-1964.[43]

Conclusion

From the very beginning, the CE movement aimed to influence young Christians by providing them with communities that were closely related to local Protestant churches. In these communities, young people's personal needs were heard and addressed, and they were taught how to be responsible Christians and maintain a spirituality of prayer and Bible meditation. The CE aimed to equip young Christians for a holy living, which would give witness to the love of God. Christian community and Christian witness were closely related.

The CE emerged in the context of a congregational church in North America and integrated easily in congregational churches in other settings, as the case of the Christian Endeavor Union in Syria and Lebanon shows. In the context of the

[42] Dikran Khrlopian. *The Golden Book*, 154.

[43] (No Author), "Endeavor on the Move," *CHANASSER* 26:2 (1963), 23.

Middle East, the CE Union took on some unique features, such as its close connection with the Armenian Evangelicals. Within the Armenian Evangelical churches, the CE functioned as their main ministry to young people and a force of spiritual renewal through its influence on devotional life, music, and scriptural knowledge. It was a "training school" for communicant members of the Armenian Evangelical Churches. Throughout its mission and service of around 100 years, the CE Union and its societies have worked to meet the spiritual needs of the youth.

Because of the close interweaving of the CE movement with the churches and its local leadership, the CE could continue to exist during the period of decolonization. When other Protestant mission agencies were no longer permitted to maintain a presence in Syria, the work of the CE continued without hindrance. When other mission agencies decided to withdraw staff and devolve responsibilities to local churches, the CE was not concerned, as it had always been a movement carried by local leaders, who remained part of the international CE network.

In today's Middle East, the CE Union in Syria and Lebanon is facing some serious challenges and struggles. Its membership reduced during the first quarter of the 21st century. While there may be various internal reasons, the political and economic situation are the primary reasons for its present state. In Syria the civil war that started in 2011 caused many Syrian Armenians to leave the country. In addition, the unparalleled Lebanese economic crisis with the hyperinflation of its currency that started in 2019 prompted many Lebanese youth to emigrate from Lebanon. To add to those challenges, a devastating explosion took place in the port of Beirut on 4 August 2020 and destroyed large residential areas of the city. Mostly recently, an earthquake hit southeast Turkey and the north of Syria including Aleppo on 6 February 2023. The explosion and the earthquake resulted in massive destruction, including damage to the offices of the CE Union in Beirut and several churches in Beirut, Aleppo, and Kessab, where CE societies are located. Thus, there are many challenges to those who are involved in Christian spiritual and missionary work among young people in the Middle East. But, as this sketch of the history of the Christian Endeavor movement shows, it has been an important community for young people in challenging times, and it may well continue to fulfil this function for many years, "for Christ and for the church."

Martyrdom and Mission in the Middle East

Wilbert van Saane

Introduction

On 7 April 2022 Coptic priest Arsanios Wadeed was stabbed to death in the city of Alexandria. In a communiqué on its official Facebook page the Coptic Orthodox Church immediately stated that Wadeed had "committed his life to God and gave his life today in an honest martyrdom."[1] This intuitive response by the Coptic Orthodox Church, without ascertaining whether the murderer had a religious motive, demonstrates the pertinence of the concept of martyrdom for the churches of the Middle East, or at least in the Coptic Church.

Recent academic studies acknowledge the pervasiveness of martyrdom in the thought and practice of the churches of the Middle East. Matthias Vogt subtitled his overview of the recent history of Christianity in the region "between martyrdom and exodus."[2] The editors of a recent handbook on Christianity in the region even adorned the cover with an icon that depicted the martyrdom of Coptic Christians at the hands of ISIS fighters in Libya in 2015.[3]

The concept of martyrdom does not imply a quietist, passive attitude. In fact, despite the threats Christians in the Middle East face, many refuse to be labelled as a powerless and persecuted minority.[4] Instead, they designate themselves as responsible citizens of their nations, who wish to contribute to the common good. As Matthias Vogt writes, they seek "integration, political participation, and cooperation." which is "their witness, or in Greek, *martyrion*."[5] At times their contribution to society as Christians is so unwelcome to some that they are killed and they become martyrs.

The Greek term *martyria* refers to both the active witness of Christians and the violent death they sometimes suffer on account of their witness. Even on the level of semantics there is thus a close connection between martyrdom and mission. This chapter focuses on this connection of mission and martyrdom in

---

[1] 'Egypt police arrest man who reportedly stabbed Coptic priest to death in Alexandria.' *Al Ahram Online*, 8 April 2022, accessed 28 April 2022, https://english.ahram.org.eg/NewsContent/1/1233/464261/Egypt/Courts--Law/Egypt-police-arrest-man-who-reportedly-stabbed-Cop.aspx?fbclid=IwAR0HQVKvKSgs7QpiNU7imwq0ckV6Ne-9yI5aEKfy2LDqdXweq81kXOgQuSA.

[2] Matthias Vogt, *Christen im Nahen Osten: Zwischen Martyrium und Exodus* (Darmstadt: WBG, 2019).

[3] Kenneth R. Ross, Mariz Tadros, and Todd M. Johnson, eds., *Christianity in North Africa and West Asia* (Edinburgh: Edinburgh University Press, 2018).

[4] The recent paper *We Choose Abundant Life: Christians in the Middle East: Towards Renewed Theological, Social, and Political Choices* (Beirut: We Choose Abundant Life Group, 2021) calls the majority-minority discourse reductionist and advocates a model of common citizenship and diversity (see especially 10-11).

[5] Vogt, *Christen im Nahen Osten*, 17.

the Middle East in the 21st century. It argues that Christian mission, which is defined as "tell, teach, tend, transform, and treasure,"[6] may lead to martyrdom.

This chapter cites four recent instances of such missionary martyrdom, from across the Middle East. In each case, faithful mission, or at least faithfulness to the Christian church and tradition, led to the death of the witnesses. In turn, these cases of martyrdom are presented by contemporary Christian sources in such a way as to inspire mission. So, while mission may lead to martyrdom, martyrdom, likewise, often leads to mission. Tertullian's famous words *semen est sanguinis Christianorum* ("the blood of Christians is a seed") acknowledged the missionary impact of the martyrdom of early Christians and may equally be applied to Christians in today's Middle East.

After presenting the case studies, this link between martyrdom and mission is further analyzed in terms of attachment to the land, the church, and relations with adherents of other faiths. The chapter concludes with some reflections on martyrdom and ecumenical-missionary cooperation of Christians in the Middle East, and shows that martyrdom transcends the boundaries of denominations and sometimes even religions. But before taking up these tasks the concepts of Christian martyrdom and martyrology need to be further elucidated.

Martyrdom and Martyrology

In ancient Greece a *martys* was a witness in a court of law. Metaphorically, the term came to refer to someone who held certain religious beliefs, such as Christians who asserted certain claims about Jesus. How could the credibility of their claims be established? As most early Christians did not have a status or position to speak of, it was only their personal integrity that could vouch for their faith.

> It was soon seen that the only way for these 'witnesses' to persuade others of the truth was to live by the same truth themselves and show by their life and conduct that they were totally committed to the testimony they gave... This kind of witness might, of course, involve suffering or even death, and their manner of bearing these things would be a significant part of their testimony.[7]

The heart of the martyria was, therefore, not primarily the suffering and death of the martyrs, but rather the way in which they confronted them. If they comported themselves with composure, faith, and dignity under duress, torture, and mortal peril, their martyria rendered the aggressive Roman policies, which aimed at apostasy rather than death, powerless. What was cultivated in the early church was a spirituality of mission and resistance, and a readiness to pay the highest price for this. The stories of those who did indeed pay that price needed

---

[6] These five marks of mission, developed in the Anglican Communion, are explained in the introductory chapter of this volume.

[7] Anthony Harvey, Richard Finn, and Michael Smart, "Christian Martyrdom: History and Interpretation," in *Witnesses to Faith? Martyrdom in Christianity and Islam*, ed. Brian Wicker (Aldershot: Ashgate, 2006), 34-35.

telling and that is why (auto)biography became such an important genre in the early church, beginning with the account of the martyrdom of Polycarp.[8]

The attempts of the Roman Empire to eradicate the Christian communities eventually achieved the opposite and strengthened the Christians' resolve. American historian Joyce Salisbury has argued that this impact went well beyond the conversion of individuals to Christianity. Memories of martyrdom also affected the way Christians viewed their position vis-à-vis governments and other groups in society, and therefore their missionary thinking and practice.[9]

The stories of Christian martyrs were recounted in martyrological writings, composed to inspire Christian readers to persevere in faith. Salisbury distinguishes several categories of such ancient writings.[10] Letters were the most important source of knowledge about martyrs and could be by or about these martyrs. *Acta* were reports of trials of martyrs based on the recollection of witnesses, and were often edited over the centuries to suit the theological purposes of different generations. Passions were descriptions of the last days of a martyr, sometimes in the form of a diary, as in the case of Perpetua of Carthage. In addition, churches kept lists of martyrs, preserved their relics, painted frescoes, and observed festivals to remember them.

In today's Middle East martyrological documents take different forms. Social media such as Facebook and YouTube are widely used for martyrology. Posts may take the form of photographic art, short documentaries, or music videos in which specially composed songs for the martyrs are accompanied by appropriate images depicting their life and passion. Other martyrological sources are photos and other visual art works, sermons and eulogies, biographies, diaries, and reports by human rights actors. Just like the martyrologies from the early church, these documents serve theological, ecclesiological and missiological purposes. They convey views about God, the church, and the role of the church in society.

There are other common elements between the early and the contemporary church in the Middle East. Just like in the early days of Christianity, Christian communities preserve the relics of the martyrs' bodies and observe festivals in their memory and honour. They also cherish objects that were in the possession of the martyrs like their clothes or books. Just like in the early church and throughout the history of the church, the new martyrs are viewed as role models and heroes. The martyrological accounts aim to keep the memory of the martyrs alive and inspire the faithful to persevere in faith.

In the context of this paper, we are especially interested in the light these sources shed on the mission of the martyrs and the mission of the anamnestic communities. Therefore, we focus on two layers in the martyrological documents: the biography of the martyr and the response of the community. We

---

[8] T*he Apostolic Fathers, with an English Translation by Kirsopp Lake, volume I: I Clement, II Clement, Ignatius, Polycarp, Didache, Barnabas* (Cambridge, Mass.: Harvard University Press and London: William Heinemann Ltd, 1975).

[9] Joyce E. Salisbury, *The Blood of Martyrs: Unintended Consequences of Ancient Violence* (New York and London: Routledge, 2004), 1-2.

[10] Salisbury, *The Blood of Martyrs*, 3-5.

seek to answer the question whether the missionary spirituality of the martyr is carried over in the missionary spirituality of the remembering community.

In line with recent ecumenical thinking on mission from the margins, we may view martyrs as marginalized people who contribute to mission. As the World Council of Churches' (WCC) statement on mission says, "[t]hrough struggles in and for life, marginalized people are reservoirs of the active hope, collective resistance, and perseverance that are needed to remain faithful to the promised reign of God."[11]

Bonnie Penner Witherall (1971-2002)

In the following sections, four recent instances of martyrdom are presented in chronological order. They occurred in different countries in the Middle East. In our retelling of their stories, we seek, on the one hand, to show how the commitment of these martyrs to Christian mission led to their martyrdom and, on the other, how their mission and their martyrdom have been depicted in the various martyrological sources that were created after their deaths, thereby inspiring others to engage in similar forms of mission.

On 21 November 2002 American missionary Bonnie Penner Witherall was shot dead at a prenatal clinic in the city of Sidon, Lebanon, where she worked. The clinic was operated by the Christian and Missionary Alliance, one of the established evangelical denominations in Lebanon. Bonnie was 31 years old and she and her husband Gary had lived and worked in Lebanon for two years.

Penner Witherall's assassination was followed by fierce debate in local and international media, centring on the legitimacy of Christian missionary work in a predominantly Islamic and Palestinian neighbourhood. *The New York Times* reported that her death had been preceded by repeated threats and that senior members of Christian and Muslim communities in the city had urged the group to decrease their activities.[12] These discussions were rendered moot, as the perpetrator of the assassination was never brought to justice, and the motive remained unknown.

In circles of evangelical missionaries and local evangelical churches, however, Penner Witherall was remembered for her devotion to Christian mission, her renunciation of luxury and safety, and her love for the women with whom she worked in Sidon. Her husband wrote a biography entitled *Total Abandon*, in which he included excerpts from her diary.[13] Some of these fragments, which were reprinted in a tribute to her life in a volume on evangelical martyrs, show that she was keenly aware of the dangers of her work, but persevered out of love and concern for the people she served.[14]

---

[11] Jooseop Keum, ed., *Together Towards Life: Mission and Evangelism in Changing Landscapes* (Geneva: WCC Publications, 2013), 17.

[12] Neil MacFarquhar, 'American Missionary Is Shot Dead in Lebanon,' *The New York Times*, 22 November 2002.

[13] Gary Witherall and Elizabeth Cody Newenhuyse, *Total Abandon* (Tyndale House Publishers, 2005).

[14] Marvin J. Newell, *A Martyr's Grace: 21 Moody Bible Institute Alumni Who Gave Their Lives for Christ* (Chicago: Moody Publishers, 2006).

In the biography, Gary Witherall sketches the grim atmosphere in Sidon in the aftermath of the 9/11 attacks on the World Trade Center and the Pentagon. In addition, the hostility between Israel and Lebanese governmental and non-governmental actors was tangible in the city of Sidon. This geopolitical situation implied a greater risk for American evangelical missionaries, and Gary and Bonnie were aware of this; they nevertheless decided to stay.

After the death of his wife, Witherall returned to the United States. In addition to writing her biography, he took on many speaking engagements, seeking to mobilize young people for missionary work. Bonnie's alma mater, Moody Bible Institute in Chicago, was one place where her martyrdom inspired many young people to consider missionary work.[15] In his addresses Gary also called for Christian-Muslim understanding and against stereotypes of Arabs.[16]

Some years later, upon hearing of Penner Witherall's martyrdom, American singer Bill Drake composed a song entitled "Wear the Crown," in which he evokes images from the Book of Revelation such as the crown and the sea. The music video includes footage of Witherall working in the clinic and also shows a crown of thorns, connecting the death of martyrs such as Witherall to the death of Christ. The song lyrics also call others to engage in similar missionary work: "Let the mantle pass to those who're left behind. / Let the runners grasp the batons of their lives."[17]

Ragheed Ganni (1972-2007)

Ragheed Ganni was a Chaldean Catholic priest who was murdered by a terrorist group, most likely Al-Qaeda, in Iraq on 3 June 2007. Ganni was born and raised in Mosul. After obtaining a degree in civil engineering and completing his military service, he trained at the University of Saint Thomas Aquinas (the Angelicum) in Rome. He was ordained a priest in Rome in 2001 and returned to Iraq in 2003, even though he was offered positions elsewhere. He became a parish priest in Mosul and secretary to Paulos Farraj Rahho, the Chaldean Archbishop of Mosul.

In the years following the American invasion, Iraqi Christian sanctuaries, clergy, and homes were repeatedly targeted. Archbishop Rahho and Father Ganni were exposed to intimidation, threats, and violence and saw many in their community leave. In 2004, Ganni's sister was wounded in an attack on a church. In an email correspondence from 2006, Ganni wrote: "We face death every day

[15] John W. Fountain, "Death Abroad Fails to Dim Bible Students' Resolve," *The New York Times*, 23 November 2002.

[16] John Blake, "Back from the Abyss," *The Atlanta Journal-Constitution*, 2005, accessed 9 May 2022, https://www.aarweb.org/common/Uploaded%20files/Awards/2006%20Blake.pdf.

[17] Bill Drake- Wear the Crown, accessed 9 May 2022, https://www.youtube.com/watch?v=w12qQDh8jR4.

here."[18] He attempted to convey the complexity of the situation in Iraq to western audiences, and the adverse effects of the invasion for the Christian population.[19]

In a written prayer from 2006, he expressed his willingness to give his life: "I am a human being and know how weak a person is. I want you to be my strength so that I will not allow anyone to insult me in the priesthood that I hold. Help me not to weaken and surrender myself in fear for my life. Because I want to die for you, to live with you and [be] with you. Now I am ready to meet you; help me not to lose time for trial. Because I told you that I knew man, but I also said that I knew you, O my strength, my power, my hope."[20]

In spite of the danger, both Rahho and Ganni kept ministering and both paid with their lives. During the Palm Sunday mass in 2007, Ganni said: "We empathize with Christ, who entered Jerusalem in full knowledge that the consequence of His love for mankind was the cross."[21] Due to the danger it was not possible to celebrate Ascension. On Pentecost Sunday, a bomb detonated in the Holy Spirit Church, where Ganni served.

One week later, on Trinity Sunday 3 June 2007, Ganni was killed right after having celebrated the Holy Qurbana (the eucharist) in the same church, along with three subdeacons, one of whom was his cousin. According to the wife of one of the subdeacons, who witnessed the killing, the gunmen shouted: "How many times did we tell you to close the church? How many times did we tell you to stop praying in the church?" Ganni's response was: "How can I close the house of God?" Upon these words, the gunmen killed Ganni and the three others. Archbishop Rahho was abducted and killed in the spring of 2008.

Ganni is remembered as "Father Ragheed of the Eucharist." He repeatedly expressed his faith in the life-giving power of the eucharist as the sacrament of Christ's dying and rising. During a visit to Italy in 2005, he listed the attacks on Christian sites in Iraq, and he admitted that he was sometimes afraid, but said that the eucharist was a source of strength, hope, and resistance.[22]

The commitment of Ganni, Archbishop Rahho, and other clergy to their city, their land, and their community has inspired Iraqi Christians who have stayed behind. This commitment was highlighted in a documentary by the Christian

---

[18] Ed West, "Fr Ragheed Ganni's 'Miracle', an example and guide for my son's life," *Asianews*, 16 May 2014, accessed 20 June 2022, https://www.asianews.it/news-en/Fr-Ragheed-Ganni's-miracle,-an-example-and-guide-for-my-son's-life--31099.html.
[19] Andrew Doran, "A Martyr in Iraq," *The American Conservative*, 3 June 2022, accessed 20 June 2022, https://www.theamericanconservative.com/a-martyr-in-iraq/.
[20] Rody Sher, "A Priest and Martyr for the Faith: The cause for the beatification of Father Ragheed Ganni," *Catholic News Agency*, 19 August 2022, accessed 20 June 2022, https://www.catholicnewsagency.com/news/252069/a-priest-and-martyr-for-the-faith-the-cause-for-beatification-of-father-ragheed-ganni.
[21] Sandra Magister, "The Last Mass of Father Ragheed, a Martyr of the Chaldean Church," *Catholic Culture*, 5 June 2007, accessed 20 June 2022, https://www.catholicculture.org/culture/library/view.cfm?recnum=7654.
[22] "'Terrorism seeks to take away life, the eucharist gives it back,' says Iraqi priest," *Asianews*, 30 May 2005, accessed 20 June 2022, https://www.asianews.it/news-en/Terrorism-seeks-to-take-away-life,-the-Eucharist-gives-it-back,-says-Iraqi-priest-3403.html.

broadcaster Tele Lumière Noursat, in which Ganni's parents explain how he served the community and refused to leave the city of Mosul.[23] His commitment was also honoured outside the Middle East, especially in Rome. In the chapel of the Pontifical Irish College in Rome, where he resided during his studies, he is depicted holding a palm branch in a mosaic with Irish saints such as Patrick and Brigid.[24] During a Mass in 2017 Pope Francis wore the stole of Fr Ganni and his canonization cause was opened in 2018.

Frans van der Lugt SJ (1938-2014)

Father Frans van der Lugt SJ, or Abouna Francis, as he was known in Syria, was shot dead near the Jesuit house of Homs, Syria, on 7 April 2014. The city had been a battleground since May 2011, and the neighbourhood where the Jesuit house was located had been isolated by insurgent militant groups, which resulted in shortages of food, water, electricity, and medicines. Despite many opportunities to leave the area, Father Frans had insisted on staying and serving the remaining citizens. He was killed only a few days before the rebels agreed to evacuate the city and the Syrian army regained control of the city.

Van der Lugt was raised in a wealthy Dutch Catholic family. In 1959, he entered the Jesuit order. Reflecting on his vocation, he cited Charles de Foucauld, the French Trappist missionary priest who was killed in southern Algeria in 1916, who wrote about humility as the only way to live in unity with Christ and do good.[25] In 1964, Van der Lugt arrived in Lebanon to study the Arabic language and two years later he moved to Homs. He returned to Europe to study theology and psychology, and he was consecrated to the priesthood in 1971. On this occasion, he made the phrase 'empty hands' his motto: "Only with empty hands it is possible to truly give, to pass on, in such a way that the recipient does not feel inferior."[26]

After completing his doctorate in psychology, he permanently moved to Syria. He served as student chaplain and, in the 1990s, began a project called Al Ard on a plot of land outside Homs that he worked with the local community, especially with young people and people living with a disability, and which also served as a social and spiritual centre.[27] Van der Lugt also led retreats and was

---

[23] The Martyrdom of Fr. Ragheed Ganni, accessed 20 June 2022, https://www.youtube.com/watch?v=zG2qgtpiPMc.

[24] Billy Swan, "The Inspiring Witness of Fr Ragheed Ganni, Servant of God," *National Vocations Office of the Irish Catholic Bishops' Conference*, 25 November 2020, accessed 20 June 2022, https://vocations.ie/2020/11/25/the-inspiring-witness-of-fr-ragheed-ganni-servant-of-god/.

[25] Frans van der Lugt, "Geschiedenis van mijn roeping," in Paul Begheyn SJ, *Frans van der Lugt SJ (1938-2014): Bruggenbouwer en martelaar in Syrië* (Nijmegen: Valkhof Pers, 2015), 17. The translations of the quotations from this book are all mine.

[26] Frans van der Lugt, "In welk perspectief zie ik mijn priesterschap," in Begheyn, *Frans van der Lugt SJ*, 31.

[27] Daniel Silas Adamson, "Frans van der Lugt: A Dutch Priest in Homs," *BBC News*, 26 April 2014, accessed 29 August 2022, https://www.bbc.com/news/magazine-27155474.

especially known for his annual hikes with young people through the Syrian countryside. He promoted a non-dogmatic, interfaith spiritual friendship.

During the siege of Homs, Van der Lugt was the only remaining Christian clergyman in the old city, where he cared for remaining families and elderly people, delivering flour by bicycle, managing a small pharmacy, and continuing his priestly duties. He attempted to report in nuanced and unbiased ways on the fighting and the humanitarian situation.[28] In January 2014, a video was released on YouTube in which he called for urgent external help, as the humanitarian situation in Homs had become desperate. He was aware of the dangers of remaining at his post, especially since one of his confreres, Paolo Dall'Oglio SJ, had disappeared in the city of Raqqa in July 2013. Yet he chose to stay, and just before Easter 2014 he paid the price with his life.

Van der Lugt is remembered for his presence and availability, his inclusiveness and practical interfaith work, and his efforts for the most vulnerable. Shortly after his death, the American scholar of Christian-Muslim relations, Jordan Denari Duffner, created an artwork which depicts him holding a book about Zen meditation, which he regularly practised, and was adorned with the bismillah, and various other religious symbols.[29] In the recollection of Syrian Christians, he stood out as a person who loved Syria and always looked for ways ahead, rather than bemoan the hardships.[30] His younger fellow-Jesuit Tony Homsy remarked that "while most refugees risked their lives using rafts or little boats to cross the Mediterranean Sea and reach the shores of Europe, a European risked his life by remaining among us in Homs. He also died with us. Perhaps we should develop deeper roots in the Syrian soil, so that we can survive and never abandon all that is good here."[31] The Jesuits in Syria have continued humanitarian and social work among families, children, and people with mental disabilities and, in the Netherlands, others have hiked in the memory of Father Frans to raise money for this work. Five years after his death, the Jesuits of Flanders and the Netherlands developed an animated film, which presented his death as a fruitful martyrdom, connected the story of Van der Lugt to the death and resurrection of Jesus Christ, and invited the viewers to continue his work of love, "because love just keeps going; it just keeps on going."[32]

---

[28] Frans van der Lugt, "Lief en leed uit Homs," in Begheyn, *Frans van der Lugt SJ*, 63-70.

[29] The icon and the explanation of its various elements may be found on the website of the artist, accessed 29 August 2022, https://jordandenari.com/2014/05/16/fr-frans-an-icon/.

[30] Ziad Hilal SJ, "Abouna Francis," in Begeyn, *Frans van der Lugt SJ*, 88-90. See also the Kruispunt documentary in which Dema Nazha, who worked with him in the pharmacy of the Jesuit House, remarks on his presence and work for peace; accessed 29 August 2022, https://www.youtube.com/watch?v=s8mM4mFN6H8.

[31] Tony Homsy SJ, "Een heel vervelende martelaar," in Begheyn, *Frans van der Lugt SJ*, 111.

[32] "Frans van der Lugt SJ, Five Years after His Death," accessed 29 August 2022, https://jesuits.eu/news/990-frans-van-der-lugt-sj-his-last-message.

The Coptic Martyrs of Libya (2015)

Our fourth case of martyrdom concerns the 21 men who were kidnapped and beheaded by members of the Islamic State in Iraq and Syria (ISIS), a terrorist group that may be regarded as a continuation of Al-Qaeda. The beheading of the 21 took place in Libya, on the beach near the city of Sirte. ISIS released a carefully choreographed video of the execution on February 15, 2015, which was widely circulated on the internet.

20 of the victims of this gruesome execution were Coptic Orthodox Christians and one was from Ghana. 13 of the Copts came from the village of Al-Our in Upper Egypt. All were migrant workers who had come to Libya to earn a better living and support their families back home. The security situation in Libya had deteriorated following the ousting of Muammar al-Qadaffi in 2011. Several attacks on Christian targets had prompted Christian migrant workers to leave the country but some had remained and formed an easy target for violent groups.[33]

Even though it is not clear whether they were given the chance to denounce their faith, the 21 are considered martyrs by the Coptic Orthodox Church, as the video is interpreted to show that they died with the name of Christ on their lips. They were not missionaries or humanitarian workers or high-ranking clergy. Nevertheless, they lived Christian lives and were dedicated to the gospel and the church. They regularly prayed and sang together in their humble quarters, and received regular visits from Coptic priests who were designated to serve the Coptic diaspora in Libya.[34] The German author Martin Mosebach sketches the importance of the church and the liturgy in their lives.

Whoever wishes to learn about the 21 must know something about the Coptic liturgy. For them, the liturgy was the most important spiritual and aesthetic expression. They were educated by it, much more than by the few years they attended school, if they went to school at all. Six of them held the ecclesiastical office of cantor, to which they were ordained by their bishop, while others sang the liturgy only on occasion. But all of them knew the liturgy by heart, as they took part in it every Sunday and on the numerous high festivals.[35]

The violence perpetrated against the 21 was presented as a message to the Coptic Church and to Christianity at large. In the view of the members of ISIS, as expressed by their spokesman in the video, these "hostile" Coptic Christians were not devout Christians, hard workers, and faithful fathers, husbands, and sons, but "crusaders" and the Coptic Church was guilty of preventing its members from converting to Islam. The "nations of the cross" were accused of waging a great war against Islam "from the Middle Ages until the present."[36]

---

[33] Akram Habib, "Libya," in Ross, Tadros and Johnson, *Christianity in North Africa and West Asia*, 52-55.

[34] Martin Mosebach, *Die 21: Eine Reise ins Land der koptischen Martyrer* (Hamburg: Rowohlt Verlag, 2018), ebook, chapter 12. An English translation by Alta L. Price was published by Plough in 2019, but I rely here on the German edition, ebook.

[35] Mosebach, *Die 21*, chapter 13. The translation is mine.

[36] Lucien van Liere, "Conquering Rome: Constructing a Global Christianity in the Face of Terror. A Case Study into the Beheading of Twenty-One Migrant Workers in January

The Coptic Church has honoured the 21 as examples and heroes of faith for their calmness and steadfastness in the face of death. Immediately after the release of the video, they were included in the Coptic calendar of martyrs, and they are commemorated on February 15. Pope Tawadros II associated their death with the death of Christ, stating that their bodies were like kernels of wheat that had to die and be sown in the earth to bear fruit.[37] After their bodies were returned to Egypt, they were buried in a state-sponsored martyrium: the Church of the Martyrs of Faith and Homeland in Al-Our.[38] Even the body of the Ghanaian man, which remained unclaimed by his family and was released by the Libyan authorities upon the formal request of the Coptic Church, was taken to Egypt, and buried in the same church.[39]

The martyrdom of the 21 has become a subject for popular and professional iconography. In popular depictions, photos of their faces are shown with crowns and halos, and in some representations, they kneel in front of Christ rather than their executioners. This is also the case in the icon written by Tony Rezk, who included the blood mixing with the water of the Mediterranean Sea, a motif from the video, but with Christ victorious over the water. In this icon, the 21 wear not just the orange outfits given to them by their executioners but also red satchels to symbolize their martyrdom.

Perhaps more so than the other three cases, the martyrdom of the 21 has drawn interest from other churches. In the video, the executioners addressed Rome with a threat to the crusading nations. In his responses, Pope Francis focused not on the threat and antagonism of this act, but rather on the unifying and exemplary potential of the 21 martyrs. Dutch scholar Lucien van Liere perceptively writes: "While this blood oozed into the Mediterranean as crusaders' blood, at the other side of the sea their blood drifted ashore as martyrs' blood."[40]

Martyrdom and the Land

With these four cases of martyrdom in mind, the remaining section of this chapter examines how martyrdom inspires a spirituality and sense of mission in the churches of the Middle East with respect to their commitment to their lands and societies, to their churches and sacraments, and to peaceful interfaith relations, especially between Christians and Muslims.

2015," in *World Christianity: Methodological Considerations*, ed. Martha Frederiks and Dorottya Nagy (Leiden: Brill, 2020), 209-224. Martin Mosebach, *Die 21*, chapter 3.

[37] Pope Tawadros II, A Word concerning the Coptic Martyrs of Libya, *Christian Youth Channel*, 2015, accessed 19 September 2022, https://www.youtube.com/watch?v=IwFuc9NcbV4.

[38] Mostafa Salem, "Tears and joy as Egyptian Christians killed in Libya laid to rest," *Reuters*, 15 May 2018, accessed 19 September 2022, https://www.reuters.com/article/us-libya-egypt-idUSKCN1IG2JU.

[39] Nader Shukry, "Last of Libya Martyrs Comes 'Home,'" *Watani*, 4 October 2020, accessed 19 September 2022, https://en.wataninet.com/opinion/editorial/watani-marks-christmas-in-a-new-way/40653/.

[40] Van Liere, "Conquering Rome," 213.

First, the anamnestic communities make a close connection between the deaths of their beloved martyrs and the land in or for which they died. To those who remember the martyrs, they inspire a continuing love for the land and the communities who live in it. The martyrs were willing to give their lives for these lands and communities – worthy objects of the love of the Christian communities. As the death of the martyrs demonstrates, this is a love that implies vulnerability and may lead to suffering and death for those who are willing to continue the work of the martyrs. Three days after Bonnie's death, Gary Witherall publicly forgave the perpetrators during the memorial service in Sidon and made the connection between Bonnie's death and the land and people of Sidon and Lebanon:

> Some people may think the death of my wife was a waste. Bonnie and I came to Lebanon understanding only a small part of the pain this country has gone through, but we believed that coming with a message of Jesus which gives hope, love, and forgiveness would never be a waste. This is a message for hurting people in a suffering generation. And this message is worth laying down our lives for… The blood of Jesus was poured out for the sins of the world, and when Bonnie's [blood] poured across the clinic [floor] on Thursday morning, she showed the same love for the women of Sidon.[41]

Likewise, Father Ragheed Ganni repeatedly stated that he desired to stay in the city of Mosul for the sake of the city and its people, and he is remembered for this. Father Van der Lugt's project was called Al Ard, the earth, and even after he had to abandon this and restrict his movements to the city of Homs, he insisted on staying with the people and share in their fate, and was buried in the place where he ministered, the Jesuit house. In the video message he recorded in the depth of the humanitarian crisis, Van der Lugt expressed his longing for life for the community of Homs: "We love life; we do not want to drown in a sea of pain and death."[42] The 21 worked in Libya for the sake of their families and communities in Upper Egypt, and their bodies were interred in the Church of the Martyrs of Faith and Homeland, a name that could not express the connection between martyrs and their land and community better.

Some theologians ascribe a salvific and prophetic significance to the martyr's efforts and self-giving for the land and its people. Commenting on the massacre at Our Lady of Deliverance Church in Baghdad on 31 October 2010, the Lebanese Orthodox Metropolitan Georges Khodr wrote that their martyrdom sanctified the land and its people. "Their blood sanctified Iraq and lifted its righteous people up to the bosom of God. Iraq is made great through their blood, and good… God, may He be blessed and exalted, sends down His grace upon innocent blood and it speaks the truth."[43] In other writings, Khodr made a connection between martyrdom and the land with respect to Palestine and

---

[41] Witherall, *Total Abandon*, 107.

[42] "People of Homs hungry to lead a normal life, says Dutch Jesuit," *Reliefweb*, 10 February 2014, accessed 29 August 2022, https://reliefweb.int/report/syrian-arab-republic/people-homs-hungry-lead-normal-life-says-dutch-jesuit.

[43] Georges Khodr, "The Christians in the East," *An-Nahar*, 13 November 2010, accessed 2 October 2022, https://georgeskhodr.org/en/the-christians-in-the-east-13-11-2010/.

Egypt.[44] Khodr intended sanctification not as a disembodied and unconditional concept here, but rather as a deep incentive to Christians and indeed to all righteous people to live a holy and vulnerable life in their lands. Likewise, the Lebanese Orthodox theologian Georges Massouh, linked the martyrdom of the 21 to the cross of Christ and attributed redeeming value to their death.

> Yes, Christians are the People of the Word [*al-Kalima*]. They are the people of Jesus Christ and His closest friends. Thus, they are the people of woundedness, and in Arabic *al-kalm* means "wound"… they realized that they are called to be witnesses to the Word in these blessed lands, even if this requires blood, suffering, torments, and forever-open wounds… Middle Eastern Christians are called today to become words, to become wounds that wipe away the sins and transgressions of this Middle East. They heal it through their suffering in all their tragedies, wars and woes and they spread peace wherever they are found.[45]

Martyrdom and the Sacramental Presence of the Church

Second, the anamnestic communities relate martyrdom to the church and the enduring sacramental presence of the Christian communities in their lands. In other words, martyrdom in today's Middle East is not just about faithfulness to the land and people living in it, it is also about the mode of Christian presence, which is viewed as sacramental, that is as a sign of God's love in Christ. The Christian presence is not a silent presence, but speaks in the words and actions of the martyrs and those who honour and emulate them. Massouh speaks of the martyr as "a living Eucharist" and of the body of the martyr as being transformed into the body and blood of Christ, and therefore being transformed into the "Church." To Massouh, this is the justification for preserving the relics of the bodies of the martyrs and building churches over these relics that carry the names of the martyrs.[46]

The implication is that, without the sacramental presence of the church of the martyrs, something essential would be missing from the Middle East. As the Lebanese Catholic theologian Gabriel Hachem writes, "In the Eastern churches, everything is liturgical: theology, poetry, iconography, hymnography, rites, sacraments, *diakonia* (service) and fraternal charity. This practice of the mysteries allows no separation between 'being a Christian' and living as a church. This witness, to the point of martyrdom, if necessary, is the manifestation of its being."[47] Father Ganni's emphasis on the faithful celebration of the eucharist testified to this, as did the liturgical life of the 21 Coptic martyrs. Two years before his death, Father Van der Lugt reported about the celebration of Easter in besieged Homs, where a community of Christians and Muslims

---

[44] See e.g. Georges Khodr, "Jerusalem and the Glory," *An-Nahar*, 14 October 2000.

[45] Georges Massouh, "The Innocence of Islam, Not of Islamic Institutions," *Lebanon Files*, 15 February 2015, 2 October 2022, https://www.lebanonfiles.com/news/845523/.

[46] Georges Massouh, "The Body of the Martyr Is a Living Eucharist," *An-Nahar*, 12 August 2017, accessed 2 October 2022, https://araborthodoxy.blogspot.com/2017/08/fr-georges-massouh-body-of-martyr-is.html.

[47] Gabriel Hachem, "Ecclesiology," in Ross, Tadros and Johnson, *Christianity in North Africa and West Asia*, 405.

supported each other in their everyday needs and gathered in the church to pray. This text brings out the sacramental presence of the witnessing church in a deep crisis.

> We celebrated Easter. Everybody came to the mass. Death, life, resurrection. What a natural resurrection faith these people have! They fled during the bombardments. They lost everything, but not their faith in life. They can still smile, serve others, make children happy. Naked and with empty hands they have travelled through death towards new opportunities for living. Their faith is not artificial at all but wells from a deep life source that has its home in their land.[48]

The sacramental presence, which is embodied by the martyrs, is remembered and continued by the community that follows them. Georges Khodr argues that this is not optional: "The testimony of blood is mandatory for us; you do not have the right to disbelieve. You keep testifying until your blood is shed."[49]

Martyrdom and Other Faith Communities

Third, the significance of the lives and deaths of the martyrs transcends their own faith communities. In each of our four cases, the martyrs were viewed by their Christian communities as an inspiration for peaceful relations with adherents of other faiths, especially Muslims. In some of the cases, Muslims took inspiration from the lives of these martyrs. This is a paradoxical point, as the killings of these martyrs happened explicitly or implicitly in the name of Islam. Despite that, the communities of the martyrs did not respond to the violence by disparaging the Islamic religion or with calls for retaliation. On the contrary, they expressed a longing for justice and peaceful coexistence between Muslims and Christians in their lands.

The violent deaths of the martyrs were met with a call to peace and justice by those who remembered them. In the communities of the men from Upper Egypt, Christians and Muslims grieved together and the church called its members to avoid anger.[50] Father Van der Lugt left a legacy of interfaith friendship, which others took up and continued to promote, beginning with his own Jesuit community in Syria, which continued to work for the most vulnerable. In American evangelical circles, Penner Witherall was remembered as an exemplary missionary and her call to love enemies and not to repay evil for evil are cited in publications that commemorate her.[51] Father Ganni's death, in particular, led to deep reflections on the need for peace, justice, and freedom of religion. In 2011, the Irish Pontifical College in Rome remembered him with a prayer walk and a conference on religious freedom. The conference included an

---

[48] Van der Lugt, "Lief en leed uit Homs," 67.

[49] Georges Khodr, "Acknowledging Faith," *Raiati*, 8 July 2012, accessed 2 October 2022, https://georgeskhodr.org/en/acknowledging-faith-08-07-2012/.

[50] André Azzam, "An Egypt in mourning prays for its martyrs beheaded in Libya," *AsiaNews*, 24 February 2015, accessed 19 September 2022, https://www.asianews.it/news-en/An-Egypt-in-mourning-prays-for-its-martyrs-beheaded-in-Libya-33543.html.

[51] Newell, *Martyr's Grace*, 23.

address by the then President of the Republic of Ireland, Mary McAleese, who knew Father Ganni personally and corresponded with him at the time of his return to Iraq. President McAleese commented on the legacy that Father Ganni left.

> Fr. Ganni lived in a world where hatred always threatened to overwhelm love. That hatred took his life – obliterated it but did not obliterate love, nor did it nor could it ever obliterate his legacy. That legacy is an enduring certainty that the greatest challenge to evil is an infinite love; that love in the face of hatred is, in the end, the only thing capable of softening the hardened heart, stirring conscience and reconciling the estranged… Freedom, including religious freedom, is about taking us to a safer world of softened hearts.[52]

Conclusion

The way in which the churches remember their martyrs reflects their perception of their role and mission in their societies. The martyrs discussed in this chapter were engaged in various aspects of Christian mission: pastoral care, evangelism, education, medical work, interfaith relations, care for vulnerable groups, or simply a peaceful Christian presence. Their communities in the Middle East and elsewhere remember them for this missionary involvement, acknowledge their exemplary and even sacramental contributions, and preserve their legacies by seeking to do likewise. Mission may lead to martyrdom, but martyrdom almost inevitably leads to mission. The Lebanese Maronite theologian Antoine Al Ahmar has called this the parenetic function of the martyrs.[53]

While it is only natural that each community especially honours martyrs from their own ranks, in recent years the churches of the Middle East have also emphasized the importance of a shared remembrance of the martyrs. Especially significant was the publication of an *Encyclopedia of the Martyrs of the Churches in Asia Minor, the Middle East and North Africa*, with the blessing of the heads of the Orthodox and Catholic churches of the region.[54] Such a joint remembrance of the martyrs is also a confirmation of the common witness of the churches, as Patriarch John X of the Antiochian Orthodox Church wrote.[55] To honour the martyrs of other denominations is not easy in a region where Protestant and Catholic missions have inflicted deep wounds on the ancient faith communities. This became evident when Penner Witherall's work was criticized by local Muslim and Christian clergy right after her assassination.

Yet, as Pope Francis has repeatedly stated in recent years, the martyrs bring Christians together in an "ecumenism of blood." The Pope has held up the

---

[52] Mary McAleese, Remarks at a Conference on 'Religious Freedom, East and West,' Pontifical Irish College, Rome, 3 June 2011, accessed 14 November 2022, https://www.catholicbishops.ie/2011/06/14/religious-freedom-fr-ganni/

[53] Antoine Al Ahmar, "Le martyre dans l'enseignement de l'Église," *Bulletin de la Faculté Pontificale de Théologie de l'USEK* (Kaslik: USEK Publishing, 2017), 59.

[54] Elias Rachid Khalil, *Encyclopedia of the Martyrs of the Churches in Asia Minor, the Middle East and North Africa* [in Arabic] (Beirut: American University of Science and Technology, 2017).

[55] Massouh, "The Body of the Martyr Is a Living Eucharist."

churches of the Middle East as examples to the global church, because they are already living this ecumenism of blood. About the 21 martyrs of Libya, who have been commemorated in various ecumenical gatherings, he specifically said: "They are our saints, saints of all Christians, saints of all Christian denominations and traditions."[56] To the Pope, the love exemplified by the martyrs should move the church forward in common service and mission. In this way, as Father Antoine Al Ahmar notes, the martyrs are an element of Christian unity and they invigorate the ecumenical movement.[57]

---

[56] Video message of His Holiness Pope Francis in memory of the Coptic martyrs killed in Libya in 2015, accessed 19 September 2022, https://www.vatican.va/content/francesco/en/messages/pont-messages/2021/documents/papa-francesco_20210215_videomessaggio-martiri-copti.html.

[57] Al Ahmar, "Le martyre dans l'enseignment de l'Eglise," 63.

Notes on Contributors

Antoine Al Ahmar is a Catholic priest member of the Lebanese Maronite Order. He is Professor of Fundamental Theology at the Pontifical Faculty of Theology at the Holy Spirit University of Kaslik (Lebanon), and former Dean of Theology and former President of the University. Since 2021, he is also the Director of the Theological and Ecumenical Department at the Middle East Council of Churches.

Grace Al-Zoughbi is a Palestinian theological educator, with expertise on Arab women in theological education. After several years on the faculty at Bethlehem Bible College, including as head of the Biblical Studies Department, she now teaches at Arab Baptist Theological Seminary in Beirut, and is the accreditation officer of the Middle East and North Africa Association for Theological Accreditation. She holds a PhD in theological education from London School of Theology. She is the author of numerous articles as well as the Esther Commentary of The Arabic Contemporary Christian Commentary.

Elias El Halabi is Associate Professor of Cultural and Interreligious Studies at the University of Balamand, Lebanon. He is also the Chairperson of the Christian-Muslim Studies Center and the Director of the Sheikh Nahyan Center for Arabic Studies and Intercultural Dialogue at the University of Balamand. His research focuses on Christian-Muslim relations in modern times, conflict, dialogue and peace.

Ziad Fahed is Professor of Moral Theology and Religious Studies at the Notre Dame University – Louaize – Lebanon, where he also serves as the Director of the University Mission. He holds a Doctorate in Theology from the Catholic University of Lyon, France. His main research interests are the theology of religions and politics, interreligious dialogue, and pluralism. He is the founder and President of the Dialogue for Life and Reconciliation Organization, which promotes interreligious dialogue among young people.

Brent Hamoud lives in Beirut, Lebanon where he works in the humanitarian and development sector. He is currently a PhD candidate at the Protestant Theological University in the Netherlands and his research explores the intersections of nationality, statelessness, and theology.

John Holdsworth is a practitioner theologian, recently retired as Executive Archdeacon of the Anglican Diocese of Cyprus and the Gulf, and a former theological college principal. He has published a number of books and articles on the Bible and Communication, the most recent of which is (2023) *Hidden in Plain Sight: Unearthing and Earthing the Psalms,* Durham UK, Sacristy Press. He is Visiting Professor of Theology and Ministry at Bishop Grosseteste University, Lincoln UK.

Though originally from the United States, **Caleb Hutcherson** and his family have called Beirut, Lebanon "home" since 2008. He is an assistant professor in historical and theological studies at the Arab Baptist Theological Seminary. He also serves in various leadership roles in the humanitarian and development sector. As a theologian, Caleb engages with issues relating to faith and everyday life, exploring questions that lie at the intersection between theology, cultural practice, and social and humanitarian issues.

Asadour Manjrian is pastor of the Armenian Evangelical Emmanuel Church in Aleppo, Syria. He holds a BA in Psychology from Haigazian University and a Master of Divinity from the Near East School of Theology in Beirut. He heads the Christian Endeavor Society at the Emmanuel Church and is also a member of the executive committee of the Christian Endeavor Union in Syria and Lebanon, for which he previously worked as secretary.

Rima Nasrallah is Associate Professor of Practical Theology at the Near East School of Theology, Beirut. She is an ordained minister at the National Evangelical Church of Beirut. She is a member of the ecojustice unit of the Middle East Council of Churches. She serves on the board of the ACT Alliance.

Wilbert van Saane is Assistant Professor of Theology and Mission at the Near East School of Theology and Campus Minister and Lecturer at Haigazian University, Beirut. He is an ordained minister in the Protestant Church in the Netherlands.

Garen Yosolkanian is an agricultural engineer and theologian. He is an Archdeacon in the Armenian Orthodox Church. He is a member of the ecumenical department of the Holy See of Cilicia. He serves on committees of various ecumenical bodies, such as the Middle East Council of Churches and the World Student Christian Federation.